SCIK

D0438371

2005
SL 10/06 · 6/07
9X 3/08 · 3/10
11+ 11/10 10/11

Made
in
China

Made
in
China

---

*What Western Managers Can Learn from
Trailblazing Chinese Entrepreneurs*

Donald N. Sull

with Yong Wang

HARVARD BUSINESS SCHOOL PRESS
Boston, Massachusetts

Library of Congress Cataloging-in-Publication Data
Sull, Donald N. (Donald Norman)
    Made in China : what western managers can learn from trailblazing
Chinese entrepreneurs / by Donald N. Sull with Yong Wang.
       p. cm.
    Includes index.
    ISBN 1-59139-715-4
    1. Entrepreneurship—China. 2. Business enterprises—China.
3. International business enterprises—China. 4. China—Economic
conditions—2000– I. Wang, Yong. II. Title.
    HB615.S94 2005
    658.4'21—dc22
                                                           2005000321

The paper used in this publication meets the requirements of the American
National Standard for Permanence of Paper for Publications and Documents
in Libraries and Archives Z39.48–1992.

Dedicated to the memory of

Professor Sumantra Ghoshal (1948–2004),

who was a role model, inspiration, and

friend to a generation of management scholars.

CONTENTS

NOTE TO THE READER

THROUGHOUT THIS BOOK we have generally relied on the pinyin system for transliterating Chinese place names and personal names into English. When a company uses an alternate spelling for an individual in their official English-language documents, however, we adopt the company's preferred spelling. Following the Western convention, we place an individual's given name before his or her surname, although we have made a few exceptions for names, such as Mao Zedong, that are already familiar to Western readers in their Chinese form. In some cases, individuals mentioned in this book prefer to use their adopted Western name, and we have honored their wishes. In reporting financial data, we have converted all currencies to U.S. dollars at the exchange rate prevailing at the end of the relevant year, unless otherwise noted.

ACKNOWLEDGMENTS

I WOULD LIKE to express my gratitude to the many managers, scholars, and students who contributed to the research that underlies this book. First and foremost, however, I would like to thank Yong (Harry) Wang, a graduate of Harvard's Kennedy School of Government, who served as my research assistant throughout the project. The initial idea for this book emerged from our discussions in 2002 about the role of entrepreneurs in China's economy. Harry was invaluable in identifying companies, arranging interviews, supervising research teams based in Shanghai and Beijing, collecting and translating company documents and secondary sources in Chinese, and working with the companies to ensure the accuracy of our data and analysis. This project required multiple rounds of interviews in the United States and China, including one particularly grueling trip when we visited eighteen Chinese companies in ten different cities over three weeks. Although our workday typically began with a breakfast meeting and extended long after dinner, Harry maintained his good humor and enthusiasm throughout. Harry is a remarkable individual, and it has been a great pleasure to work with him.

This project provided the opportunity to interview several of China's most admired executives and entrepreneurs. We thank all of these managers for being so generous with their time and insights and are particularly grateful to Ying Han, Xingsheng Zhang, Ying

Wu, Johnny Chou, Ruimin Zhang, Mianmian Yang, Zhidong Wang, Chuanzhi Liu, Mary Ma, Yaochang Yu, Qinghou Zong, Zongnan Wang, Boquan He, and Charles Zhang.

We are grateful to James Z. Li, managing director of E. J. McKay in Shanghai, and Min Zhao, chairman of Sinotrust in Beijing. Jim and Min helped arrange access to companies and schedule interviews. They also hired teams of analysts in Shanghai and Beijing to collect, analyze, and translate data, including information on corporate financial and operating performance, chronologies of key events for the companies we studied, industry and regulatory information, and competitive profiles. These detailed analyses influenced our selection of companies and provided the basis for structuring interview questions. We are deeply grateful to Jim and Min for their financial support in hiring the research teams, their help in arranging interviews, and their personal insights into the Chinese business environment. Special thanks go to Yang Yang at Sinotrust and to Christine Ma and Caroline Rowe at E. J. McKay, who led the local research teams in Beijing and Shanghai, respectively.

Several MBA students from the Harvard Business School graduating class of 2004 contributed to this research, and we are deeply indebted to them for their hard work in researching and writing detailed case studies of selected companies in our sample. Aaron Wen and Nelson Liu worked with Harry to write a case study of Ting Hsin; Ying Zhang, Liyang Jin, and Yong Yuan researched and wrote a case on Wahaha; Jason Hu, Charles Xu, Allen Qian, and Julia Zheng completed a case on UTStarcom. Xi Zhang, Soo Chuen Tan, and Seth Wheeler shared findings from their research into China's microwave oven industry. My former student Greg Ye (Harvard Business School class of 2001) provided valuable input based on his in-depth case study of Legend written with Henry Chen, Harry Qin, Zheng Yin, and Michael Rukstad. Numerous Chinese students at the Harvard Business School shared their insights throughout the project, and we are grateful for their help. Michael J. Roberts, executive director of Harvard's Arthur Rock Center for Entrepreneurship, collaborated to revise his earlier case study on AsiaInfo. We acknowledge financial support from the Harvard Business School's Division of Research and from the London Business School.

Several experts on Chinese history and economics graciously took the time to review our manuscript in part or whole and provide detailed feedback. We would like to thank in particular Professor Laixiang Sun of the School of Oriental and African Studies (SOAS), University of London; Professor Dic Lo, also of SOAS; Professor Lin Xu of Babson College; and Yingpu Qu, an Edward S. Mason Fellow at Harvard's Kennedy School of Government. We are grateful to managers within the companies we studied who reviewed relevant chapters for factual accuracy, and also to Simon Israel of Danone, who provided his insights on China's food and beverage sector. In addition, we would like to thank others who provided valuable input, including Miao Cao (World Bank), Xiaoqing Ding (Merrill Lynch), Frank Fan (Cambridge Partners), Jinyue Gao (Bank of China), George Lu (Surfmax Investments), Xiaobo Wu (author), Xiaodong Yi (Sullivan & Cromwell), Xin Zhou (Deutsche Bank), Weimin Zhou (Beijing Investment Promotion Bureau), Xiaogang Tan (Ministry of Finance), and especially Christina Zhu (McKinsey), Professor Waverly Ding (UC Berkeley), and Professor Tao Zhu (Cornell). We are grateful for the insights of Sheree Chuang of Commonwealth Publishing, who conducted in-depth research into Ting Hsin and Uni-President. Charles Spinosa provided valuable insights on Haier.

Made in China

Meet the Players

THE STORIES of America's iconic entrepreneurs are well known. Hundreds of books are devoted to business builders such as Bill Gates, Michael Dell, Sam Walton, and Henry Ford, while thousands more mention them.[1] Western readers know virtually nothing, however, about the leading entrepreneurs in the world's second-largest economy—China. That is a shame on several dimensions.

China is, of course, a critical driver of the global economy. It's obviously big—nearly equal in size to the United States and home to one of every five people on the planet. Since economic reforms in the late 1970s, China's economic growth has been astounding.[2] GDP quadrupled from 1978 to 2002, and by 2003, China was the second-largest economy in the world after the United States, when measured in terms of purchasing power. Some credible analysts believe China's economy could overtake America's by 2045, within the lifetime of many people reading this book.[3] If the country's provinces were classified as separate economies, Chinese provinces would have accounted for twenty of the world's thirty fastest-growing economies between 1978 and 1995, according to World Bank estimates. China leads the world in attracting foreign direct investment and in the production of mobile phones, color televisions, microwave ovens, and air conditioners, among other products. China is also one of the largest importers of raw materials, with the country's enormous appetite for inputs contributing to the rise of oil prices, for example. The list could go on, but the point is simple. It's odd that we know so little about the entrepreneurs reshaping the second-largest and arguably most dynamic economy in the world.

Many subjects—macroeconomics and accounting come to mind—are important but dull. China's recent history, however, has been both significant and fascinating. China essentially eliminated entrepreneurship for a generation, and then let it loose again beginning in the late 1970s. The unleashing of entrepreneurial energy that followed represents one of the most important events in recent economic history. The process has been a roller coaster ride for many of the entrepreneurs at the vanguard of China's charge into the market economy. Since 2000, *Forbes* magazine has published a list of China's wealthiest people, which documents the rise of entrepreneurs who built great fortunes in the span of only a few years. The list also chronicles the rapid fall of high fliers, with approximately 30 percent of the individuals tumbling off the list each year, and more than a few ending up in prison. The entrepreneurial fervor of China today recalls the bare-knuckled capitalism of the Industrial Revolution in the United States, when men like Henry Ford, John D. Rockefeller, and Andrew Carnegie amassed tremendous fortunes by navigating through a rapidly changing economy.

Understanding China's entrepreneurs is also critical for managers whose companies look to China as a source of future growth. China is a huge and growing market that few companies can ignore, but it has also proven a devilishly difficult place to make money. Many highly admired Western companies, such as Microsoft and Wal-Mart, have found the Chinese market a hard nut to crack. Several factors make conducting business in China difficult, including unclear intellectual property protection, regulatory obstacles, and distribution bottlenecks. The strength of homegrown competitors, however, ranks high on the list of competitive challenges.[4] Even global brand leaders such as Procter & Gamble and Coca-Cola have encountered stiff competition from local brands in China. Western managers who understand their Chinese rivals are less likely to underestimate them as future rivals and will be better equipped to compete against them.

Chinese entrepreneurs can also serve as critical partners for Western firms attempting to crack the Chinese market. Western companies that find the right partner, strike a good deal, and manage the resulting partnership with Chinese entrepreneurs can often turbocharge their results. Consider the French food group Danone, which booked over $1 billion in revenues in China in 2003. The company succeeded not by going it alone, but rather by forging a series of partnerships with leading entrepreneurs, most notably the Hangzhou Wahaha Group, which leads China's bottled water market. The Chinese partners benefited from Danone's capital, technology, and marketing expertise, while Danone leveraged these entrepreneurs' knowledge of local consumers.

Lessons on Competing in an Unpredictable World

China's entrepreneurs provide valuable lessons on managing effectively in an unpredictable context. Of course, no entrepreneurs can easily profit or sustain superior performance in any market in the world: customers demand more for less, competitors imitate a company's success formula, and substitute products or services threaten to steal customers. Succeeding in China is tougher still. Besides the usual challenges, Chinese companies face extremely high levels of uncertainty across multiple dimensions. Each of these variables is individually uncertain, and their interactions make the future nearly impossible to predict with any degree of confidence. With limited visibility into the future, executives in China must anticipate and react quickly to a constantly changing environment. In addition to the competitive, technological, and customer uncertainty facing every business, the following factors further increase unpredictability in China.

- *Unpredictable regulation and industrial policy.* Every industry in China is subject to abrupt changes in regulations that
  can profoundly influence firms' competitive position and
  financial performance. In some cases these shifts result from
  jockeying among competing agencies with overlapping policy
  responsibilities. For example, in June 2003, in a bid to lower
  bank exposure to an overheating real estate market, the
  People's Bank of China (China's central bank) issued guidance to commercial banks to restrict loans to real estate
  developers and homebuyers, effectively starving real estate
  firms of their primary source of funding. Industry experts
  predicted a large percentage of real estate firms would exit
  the industry, and indeed many did. Three months later, however, the State Council—the highest executive organ of state
  power, composed of leading party officials—reaffirmed government support for the real estate industry, announced a different policy interpretation, and recommended that commercial banks continue to issue loans to qualified real estate
  developers as they saw fit.[5]

  Even when there is no conflict among national agencies,
  central governmental edicts are subject to local interpretation
  and enforcement. As a result, uncertainty about nationwide
  regulations is aggravated by differences in how they are
  implemented across regions. In 2001, for example, a national
  tax was introduced on beverage consumption. Regional officials in the Sichuan and Guizhou provinces strictly enforced
  the tax, which reduced local beverage companies' profits by
  over 20 percent. Other provinces, however, failed to enforce
  similar duties. As a result, beverage companies in those two
  provinces paid 97 percent of the consumption tax collected
  that year across all China, although their sales accounted for
  less than 14 percent of the national total. Their profits, ability
  to invest, and competitive position suffered, of course.[6]

- *Uncertainty from integration into global markets.* Although
  Chinese competitors have attracted the attention of Western
  managers in recent years, in many cases Chinese firms have

been exposed to the vagaries of global product, technology, and labor markets for decades. Entry into global markets created new opportunities for exports, but also left firms vulnerable to foreign tariffs and import restrictions. The opening of the Chinese markets has exposed Chinese entrepreneurs to the onslaught of deep-pocket multinationals on their home turf, which further increased unpredictability.

Access to global technology markets injected further uncertainty into the game. Lacking a domestic technology base, Chinese companies in many industries must rely on technology developed and controlled by multinational rivals, placing both access and licensing fees outside their control. The alliance that controlled the core DVD technology, for example, initially demanded significant licensing fees from Chinese DVD manufacturers, and only reached agreement on a reasonable fee after several rounds of prolonged negotiations.[7]

- *Uncertain access to and cost of capital.* China's state-run banks have historically allocated funds to state-owned enterprises, which found their funding tied to compliance with shifting policy initiatives. Vibrant private companies, in contrast, could only secure loans periodically. Access to funding for private companies has historically been sporadic, and the cost of capital has fluctuated dramatically. Domestic securities markets have failed to provide a reliable alternative to banks because of widespread price manipulation, limited liquidity, and the large overhang of government-owned shares that could be sold on the market at any time. Some Chinese firms have been able to access global capital markets, but fall in and out of favor with international investors. Entrepreneurs cannot be assured that access to global capital markets will coincide with periods when they need funds.

Although many Chinese entrepreneurs have relied on foreign direct investment, access to this capital has not been consistent over time or across provinces. In 1989, for example, many multinationals in the telecommunications industry abruptly reduced their investment in China in the wake of the

Tiananmen Square turmoil. Fierce regional competition for foreign direct investment among local governments also results in rapid shifts in the level of foreign capital available to firms within any one city or province.

Private entrepreneurs have devised an impressive array of informal financing mechanisms, including interest-free interpersonal lending, rotating credit associations, and institutionalized financial intermediaries such as private money houses and credit cooperatives.[8] Although creative, these mechanisms fail to provide predictable access to capital at reasonable cost.

- *Macroeconomic jolts.* Although China's currency has been pegged to the dollar at a fixed exchange rate since 1993, it was subject to sharp changes in value prior to that (see figure 1-1 for historical exchange rates). The renminbi experienced sharp devaluations relative to the dollar in the late 1980s and again in the mid-1990s. The changes in exchange rates create new opportunities for exporters and new threats for companies that pay for raw materials, technology licenses, or interest expenses in dollars. Rapid growth in the Chinese economy has also triggered central bank increases in interest rates to cool down the economy. Although the country's macroeconomic situation has been stable compared with Latin American and Eastern European markets, it remains volatile by the standards of most Western economies.

- *Unclear and shifting property rights.* Murky property rights introduce significant uncertainty regarding the basic question of who owns which assets of a business. Many Chinese entrepreneurs began their companies as affiliates of state entities such as townships, villages, or schools. Over time, equity has transferred to entrepreneurs, employees, and investors, but in many cases the basic question of who owns what remains unclear. Lack of clarity regarding property rights makes it difficult for businesses to provide incentives and enter into binding contracts governing the use of assets.

FIGURE 1-1

Chinese yuan renminbi per dollar at year end: 1984–2004

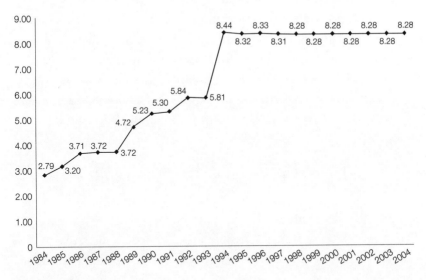

Source: Bank of China.

China's evolving intellectual property (IP) regime has left many multinationals reluctant to transfer their latest generation of technology to China and made it difficult for local companies to access technology. Evolving IP regulations also limit domestic companies' ability to predict the returns they will earn on any investment in research and development.

Despite these obstacles, an elite group of Chinese companies managed not only to survive, but to thrive amidst the unpredictability that characterized China's move to a market economy and integration into the global economy. The successful companies we studied responded quickly and effectively to shocks that threatened their very survival and forced less successful competitors out of business. They quickly seized major opportunities that positioned them well for the future.

This book distills general insights about succeeding in unpredictable markets based on our observations of the Chinese entrepreneurs we studied, and codifies them into general principles that can be used by any manager facing an unpredictable future. This book is part of a multiyear research program studying the principles of effective management in various unpredictable environments, including airlines, enterprise software, medical devices, and emerging markets (i.e., China and Brazil).[9] The principles in this book align with findings from research on successful companies in other unpredictable markets, including those emerging markets described in Donald N. Sull and Martin Escobari, *Success Against the Odds: What Brazilian Champions Teach About Thriving in Unpredictable Markets*.[10]

Introduction to the Companies

Attempting to analyze all of China's entrepreneurs across every sector would prove an impossible task. To focus our research, we selected four sectors: information technology, telecommunications equipment and services, food and beverage, and white goods (i.e., appliances). (See the appendix for a detailed explanation of our research design and methods.) These industries provided several advantages: they were among the first industries in China to integrate into global markets, had evolved to the point where more and less successful players could be distinguished, were sufficiently large that credible data were available, and provided diversity along several dimensions, including technology intensity, number of customers served, and relative importance of exports. Of course, four sectors could not possibly capture the breadth of Chinese economic activity, but these industries provide some variety.

Within each industry, we chose companies through a rigorous selection process. We narrowed a list of over sixty firms across the four sectors based on analysis of financial and market performance, surveys with industry experts, published company rankings, and interviews. We selected companies to achieve diversity along multiple dimensions, such as background of the founder, size of firm, ownership structure, level of diversification, and location, including firms headquartered in some of the most dynamic economic regions of

China including Beijing, the Yangtze River Delta, and the Pearl River Delta. The diversity of industry and firms not only provided a rich overview of China's entrepreneurs, but also increased our confidence that the insights we gleaned were not idiosyncratic to a specific region, industry, or organizational form.

Our final eight companies are Legend and Sina in information technology, UTStarcom and AsiaInfo in telecommunications equipment and service, Haier and Galanz in appliances, and Wahaha and Ting Hsin in food and beverages. When possible, we paired each of our eight focal companies with a comparable firm that was less successful, which provided a valuable contrast. (See table 1-1 and the following list for a summary of the firms.) Let us be perfectly clear— we studied these entrepreneurs and companies because they succeeded in the past, but we are under no illusions that past success guarantees superior performance in the future. Any one of the firms we studied could stumble if it lets its guard down in the future. For example, we already see signs that Legend and Haier face enormous

TABLE 1-1

Overview of companies

Company	Line of business	Headquarters region	Comparison company
Information technology			
Legend (Lenovo)	Personal computer	Beijing	Great Wall
Sina Corp.	Internet portal	Shanghai	InfoHighway
Telecommunications equipment and services			
UTStarcom	Telecom equipment	Hangzhou	None
AsiaInfo	Telecom services	Beijing	None
White goods			
Haier	Home appliances	Qingdao	Red Star
Galanz	Microwave ovens	Shunde	SMC
Food and beverage			
Wahaha	Beverages	Hangzhou	Robust
Ting Hsin	Noodles, beverages	Tianjin/Taipei	Uni-President

challenges in sustaining profitable growth as competition increases from both domestic and foreign competitors. Ting Hsin's diversification has overextended the group's resources, in our assessment, and left the group vulnerable going forward. These companies succeeded in the past by following the principles described in this book. If they fail to do so in the future, however, they are likely to fail. Unpredictable markets are merciless, and the notion of companies "built to last" is a dangerous myth.

- *Legend Group Ltd.* Founded in 1984, Beijing-based Legend (known by the Lenovo brand outside China since 2004) is the largest information technology company in the People's Republic of China, with revenues of $3 billion in fiscal year 2004 and employing nearly 10,000 people. Its branded personal computer (PC) has been the country's best-selling PC since 1997, with a market share of over 27 percent at year-end 2003. Legend was also the number one PC brand in Asia Pacific (including Japan), with a regional market share of 12.6 percent, and is among the top ten computer companies in the world. In recent years, Legend has entered into several new market segments, including online services, information technology consulting, and mobile phone handsets; these new businesses have started to increase their contribution to the company's financial performance.

- *Sina Corporation.* With 2003 revenues of $114 million and net profits of $31 million, Shanghai-based Sina hosts China's leading Internet portal and was ranked the country's most popular online destination in 2003. Sina translated its traffic into leadership among online advertisers and led China's portals in providing value-added services such as news and horoscopes as short message services (SMS) over mobile phones in recent years. At year-end 2003, China's 80 million Internet users represented the second-largest market in the world, and some analysts expected the country to overtake the United States in Internet users by 2008. Sina also targeted Chinese speakers globally with its Mandarin-language Web sites serving mainland China, Hong Kong, Taiwan, and North America. Many users consider Sina the most reliable source of online news in Chinese.

- *Haier Group.* Headquartered in Qingdao (the same city that produces Tsingtao beer), Haier is the leader of China's home appliance market, with a 30 percent market share and 2003 revenues of $9.7 billion. Founded in 1984, the company currently employs approximately 30,000 people. Worldwide, the company is ranked fifth among all appliance manufacturers and is second only to Whirlpool in refrigerator unit sales. The story of Haier's rise is legendary in China, and it is the Chinese company that Western readers are most likely to recognize. Since the mid-1980s, the company has expanded its product range from refrigerators to a wide variety of white goods, including air conditioners, microwaves, and vacuums, as well as consumer electronics such as mobile phones and televisions. Haier exports to more than 150 countries globally and has 22 production facilities and 18 design centers outside China. In 2003, Haier ranked number one among the most admired Chinese companies.

- *Guangdong Galanz.* Although not as well known as Haier, Guangdong Galanz has carved out a commanding leadership in China's microwave oven sector. It has the leading market share in every major Chinese city where it competes, outselling the second-largest brand (which varies by city) by a multiple of two to six times unit volume. The company has over 20,000 employees and 2003 revenues of $1.3 billion. Galanz built upon its position in China to become the global leader in unit production of microwave ovens, with annual output exceeding 16 million units in 2003. Galanz estimates that its share of global microwave oven unit production was over 40 percent in 2003, with its share in certain emerging markets in South America and Africa exceeding 70 percent of units sold. The vast majority of these units are manufactured for sale under other companies' brands. In 2001, the company diversified into air conditioner production and declared its intention to become the world's number one producer of air conditioners.

- *UTStarcom.* Founded in 1995 through the merger of two telecommunications start-ups headquartered in the United States but focused on the Chinese market, UTStarcom has grown its revenues from $10 million in 1995 to $2 billion in 2003, a performance that landed UTStarcom a place on the 2003 *Fortune* 1000. UTStarcom achieved its rapid growth by developing and selling its "Personal Access System," which enables cordless phones to rove up to 60 miles within a city limit. At the end of 2003, UTStarcom's equipment served over 20 million customers in China, and the company exported telecommunications equipment to emerging markets such as India and to developed countries, including Japan and the United States. The company, which employs approximately 5,000, trades on the NASDAQ exchange and had a market capitalization exceeding $4 billion in September 2004.

- *AsiaInfo Holdings.* Founded in 1994, AsiaInfo's products and services cover telecommunications network infrastructure and services, including messaging, customer relationship management, and billing solutions. AsiaInfo has built most of mainland China's Internet infrastructure, designing and building the country's first national commercial Internet backbone (ChinaNet) in 1995 as well as its first provincial Internet backbone (GuangdongNet). The company has approximately 900 employees and reported revenues of over $121 million in 2003.

- *Hangzhou Wahaha Group.* Founded in 1987, Wahaha today is the leading beverage producer in China, accounting for approximately 15 percent of the country's total beverage production by volume, and ranks number five among global beverage companies. Based in Hangzhou, the company employs approximately 10,000 people and reported $1.2 billion in revenues in 2003. Despite fierce competition from local rivals

and multinationals including Coke, Pepsi, and Danone,
Wahaha emerged as China's market share leader in bottled
water, fruit-flavored milk, and congee (a traditional rice por-
ridge eaten throughout China as a breakfast food); competed
in ready-to-drink tea and bottled fruit juices; and had established itself as a viable third player in the carbonated beverage market, after Coke and Pepsi.

- *Ting Hsin Group.* Founded in 1958 as a small oil plant in
Taiwan, Ting Hsin has made substantial progress toward
achieving its vision of becoming a leading food group in
greater China. Tingyi—the group's publicly listed subsidiary
that traded on the Hong Kong stock exchange—reported
2003 revenues of $1.3 billion and had an enterprise value of
$1.9 billion at the end of that year. The Tianjin-based Tingyi
controlled Master Kong, one of the best-recognized consumer
brands in China, and an extensive distribution network that
included 344 sales offices serving nearly 5,000 wholesalers
and 50,000 retailers throughout mainland China. At the end
of 2003, Tingyi was the leader in China's market for instant
noodles, with 44 percent share of market by value; ready-
to-drink tea, with 47 percent market share; and sandwich
crackers, with nearly one-quarter of the market. In addition
to its stake in Tingyi, the Ting Hsin Group also controlled
Wei Chuan (Taiwan's second-largest food company) as well
as Hymart (a chain of hypermarket and shopping malls in
China), Buynow (a large personal computer retailer in
Beijing), and DICOS (a fast-food chain with over 200 stores
in China).

A Brief Overview
of Recent Chinese History

To appreciate the accomplishments of the entrepreneurs in this book,
one must understand the events they lived through, which provided
the backdrop against which they founded and grew their companies.

We cannot hope to do justice to the complex and fascinating history of modern China in a few pages, and we don't try. Instead, we touch on some of the key events that are essential to making sense of the stories we discuss in subsequent chapters.[11] Readers interested in exploring Chinese history in greater depth can turn to many outstanding books that we used as sources in preparing our short history.[12]

Few people realize it, but China was the only political and economic superpower in the world for hundreds of years. As recently as 1820, China accounted for approximately 30 percent of global GDP, approximately the same percentage as the United States currently contributes.[13] During the nineteenth century, China suffered a prolonged decline, culminating in the collapse of the Qing Dynasty in 1911 after nearly three centuries of rule. As the Qing Dynasty dissolved and in the period thereafter, foreign powers eyed China as a candidate for colonization, which led to a series of foreign incursions beginning in 1840 and culminating in Japanese annexation of northern China during the Sino-Japanese War of 1937 to 1945. The collapse of the Qing Dynasty also resulted in fragmentation of the nation into feuding states, with local warlords engaging in incessant struggles for land and resources.

The Civil War (1927–1949)

During the chaotic years after the collapse of the Qing Dynasty, two key political parties emerged: The Kuomintang, or Nationalist Party, founded in 1912, and the Communist Party of China founded nine years later. The Nationalists and Communists initially cooperated until the right-wing General Chiang Kai-shek gained the upper hand in 1927 and purged the Communists, beginning a Chinese civil war that extended for over two decades (although the two parties collaborated for several years to battle the Japanese).

The Nationalists proceeded to win territory in northern and eastern China from local warlords, while the Communists retreated to rural areas. General Chiang led a series of campaigns to destroy the Communists, and during the fifth campaign had the Communists on the ropes. Facing the prospect of complete annihilation in 1934, the

Communists, led by Mao Zedong and Zhou Enlai, set off on the Long March—a yearlong advance covering several thousand miles through some of China's most formidable terrain. (Throughout this book we follow the Western convention of placing Chinese forenames before surnames, except in cases where the Chinese name is already familiar in the original sequence.) Of the ninety thousand troops that began the journey, only a fraction survived the Long March, but these hardened veterans provided the core of what would later become the People's Liberation Army. The time spent in Yan'an in the remote northwestern province of Shaanxi allowed the Communist Party to regroup under the leadership of Mao.

The Communists and Nationalists suspended their hostilities between 1936 and 1945, when the Chinese fought to drive Japanese troops out of the country. After the expulsion of the Japanese, however, fighting between the Communists and Nationalists resumed with renewed fury. U.S. General George Marshall attempted to broker a truce, but neither the Communists nor Nationalists were willing to cede territory, and the failed talks were followed by intensified conflict. Although the Nationalist government possessed a large army, controlled significant land, and received support from the United States, economic mismanagement had resulted in hyperinflation, and corruption eroded the party's legitimacy and popular support. Building on their strong position in rural areas, the Communists defeated the Nationalists, who retreated in 1949 with approximately 2 million loyalists to the island of Taiwan. The triumphant Communist Party founded the People's Republic of China in that same year.

Early Success and the Great Leap Forward (1949–1960)

Under the leadership of Mao, the Communists undertook to fundamentally transform the new nation in one of the most far-reaching experiments in social engineering in human history. Building on the Soviet model, China's Communist Party began to implement large-scale socialist reforms of the economy: industry was nationalized, agriculture collectivized, and many large-scale infrastructure projects launched. Impressed by the early success of the Soviet Union, China's Communist leaders instituted the country's first five-year plan in 1953—a top-down plan to stimulate rapid industrialization and economic progress.

Encouraged by the country's economic advances in the first few years of Communist rule, Mao planned to leap over the development stages through which Western economies had progressed on their way to industrialization. In 1958, Mao initiated the Great Leap Forward to mobilize China's ample supply of inexpensive labor to produce steel, the commodity most closely associated with industrialization. To avoid importing heavy machinery, peasants were required to abandon their fields and build small steel furnaces in their backyards that produced cast iron from scrap metal (and in some cases farming implements). The backyard smelting rapidly expanded beyond peasants, and soon factory workers, teachers, and doctors abandoned their work to produce scrap iron in makeshift facilities. The redeployment of farmers to inefficient steel production, aggravated by unfavorable weather conditions, led to widespread famine throughout China.

When the Great Leap ended in 1960, the resulting famine (at one time referred to as the "Great Leap famine") is estimated to have killed approximately 30 million people directly, and ranked among the greatest famines in human history.[14] Facing the failure of the Great Leap policies, economic pragmatists in the Communist Party led by Yun Chen, Shaoqi Liu and Xiaoping Deng terminated most of the programs and reestablished economic policies that had worked prior to the Leap.

The Cultural Revolution (1966–1976)

Based on their success in restoring economic progress, pragmatists such as Chen, Deng, and Liu increased their standing among Party members and the general population and planned to promote Mao to a figurehead position while limiting his influence on policy. Mao had other plans, however, and launched the Great Proletarian Cultural Revolution in 1966, in which he exhorted teenagers—known as Red

Guards—to maintain the progress of the socialist revolution by purging the country of anyone who resisted the movement and by destroying relics of China's pre-Communist history. In August of that year, Mao assembled several million Red Guards from around China and encouraged them to purge the country of obstacles to the socialist revolution and wrest power from the Communist Party apparatus.

Emboldened by Mao's exhortation, the teenaged Red Guards went on a rampage through the country. Supposed enemies of the state, including Communist Party officials, professionals, and the Red Guards' teachers, were routinely humiliated, tortured, and executed by the Red Guards without any semblance of a trial. The Red Guards also set about systematically destroying all vestiges of China's culture, looting and tearing down temples and monuments and burning ancient texts and art in bonfires. Mao praised these actions and issued an edict barring police officers from intervening to control the Red Guards. Mao also dealt with his political rivals, sending Liu to a prison camp and exiling Deng to work in a factory (Chen had earlier left the public stage by taking a sick leave that lasted until after Mao's death). To maintain a direct link to the Red Guards, Mao encouraged them to make a pilgrimage to Beijing for direct instructions and encouragement from him, with the government subsidizing all expenses for the trips.

The chaos of the Cultural Revolution unleashed bitter political infighting from the top of the Communist Party to the smallest village. Government officials seized on the Cultural Revolution as a means to eradicate their political rivals, while competing Red Guard factions contended for power. Red Guards were even encouraged to replace the People's Liberation Army and loot military facilities, while generals for a time were ordered to permit these attacks (although this policy was quickly reversed). In 1968, Mao began to create a cult of personality through the publication of the "Little Red Book," which collected many of his quotations in a single source for Red Guards to memorize and use to inform their actions.

In 1968, Mao also initiated the Down to the Countryside Movement, in which Red Guards and other young intellectuals, including college students, scientists, professionals, and children of educated parents, were relocated to remote rural areas to receive "reeducation" at the hands of peasants. This policy, which remained in force for nearly a decade, was intended not only to instill peasant virtues in intellectuals but also to contain the unrest led by the Red Guards and remove potential opponents to Mao's reforms. The Cultural Revolution and the relocation to rural areas deprived many of China's best and brightest, including a few of the entrepreneurs we studied, of professional opportunities to match their ambition and talent.

Although the most extreme policies were promulgated in the period between 1966 and 1968, the leaders of the Cultural Revolution maintained their power until Mao's death in 1976, preventing a generation of professionals and intellectuals from pursuing their careers, while basic services, including health care, education, and transportation, deteriorated. Despite the economic and social disruption to Chinese society in this period, the dislocation of the Cultural Revolution resulted in a de facto decentralization of economic decision making; the managers of state-owned enterprises could run their businesses outside the scope of centralized planning.[15] Free of the planned economy, many rural enterprises grew rapidly during the 1970s.[16] The hardships of the Cultural Revolution also produced a generation of potential entrepreneurs inured to hard work and hardship, favoring pragmatism over theory, and eager to pursue opportunity. In many respects, the Cultural Revolution cultivated the generation of entrepreneurs whose pent-up energy and drive were unleashed during the economic reforms that followed.

Economic Liberalization (1978–1989)

After the turmoil of the Cultural Revolution, China's economy stood on the brink of collapse. In the late 1970s, however, Xiaoping Deng managed to outmaneuver Mao's handpicked successor, consolidate his power base, and emerge as China's leader. After repudiating the Cultural Revolution, Deng set about a double-pronged approach to economic reform, which entailed shifting from central planning to a more market-oriented system and opening China to the global economy. China's political leadership relinquished the niceties of ideology for results in formulating and implementing its economic policy. As Deng famously remarked, "It does not matter whether the cat is white or black; if it catches mice, it is a good cat."

One of the most important reforms was the creation of three Special Economic Zones located in Guangdong province (Shenzhen, Zhuhai, and Shaotou) and one in Fujian province. These zones drew foreign direct investment and technology into China by providing tax incentives to joint ventures between Chinese entities and multinationals, established to export goods that would earn foreign currency. The zones enjoyed wide discretion in setting trade policies, tax regulations, land use, and business approval procedures, all exempt from the central planning process. The success of these initial experiments led Beijing to allow other provinces such latitude, and in 1984, fourteen more cities were added. The reform of state universities and research institutes, moreover, spawned several technology start-ups.

Deng also reformed agriculture, by replacing communal farming with a system that allowed households to decide which crops to plant, to sell their produce, and to retain the proceeds from their sale. This system proved much more effective than the communal farming it replaced, and agricultural output improved dramatically. Total domestic grain production, for example, increased from 305 million tons in 1978 to 394 million tons in 1988 without any significant improvement in technology.[17] The success of agricultural reform improved farmers' disposable income and increased support among farmers for further economic reform. One such innovation was the rise of township and village enterprises, new ventures owned and funded by government bodies, such as schools, or collectively owned by workers that pooled their capital to underwrite the new enterprises. This organizational form allowed entrepreneurs to secure funding and employees for start-ups. The number of township and village enterprises in China rose from 1.5 million in 1978 to 19 million in 1991, by which time they employed approximately 96 million people and played a pivotal role in Chinese economic development.[18] These enterprises provided an opportunity for China's first generation of entrepreneurs, many of whom had been relegated to manual labor during the Cultural Revolution.

Resuming Growth After Tiananmen Square (1989 to the Present)

Deng's pragmatism allowed China to avoid the ideological debate that had crippled economic progress during Mao's reign. Not surprisingly, given the scale of the endeavor, economic reform weathered its share of ups and downs, with the leadership periodically issuing conflicting signals or retightening control. The economic reform agenda halted abruptly when the turmoil in Tiananmen Square in 1989 culminated in the military suppression of protesters. The Tiananmen incident brought on international economic sanctions, sending China's economy into decline, and resulted in a reshuffling at the top of the Communist Party that many interpreted as signaling a rise of conservatives more interested in stability than economic reform.

In 1992, however, Deng injected new momentum into the process of economic reform. Deng, officially retired, toured southern China as a private citizen to inspect the region's economy and reaffirm the regime's ongoing commitment to market reforms and opening up to the global economy. The widely publicized tour emboldened southern entrepreneurs and gave China's stalled economy a fillip. The pace of reform again accelerated, and in 1993 a revision of China's constitution called for the development of a "socialist market economy" in which the Communist Party would retain political power while encouraging a free market economy. The 1990s heralded important economic changes in China, including the reform of many state-owned enterprises, the privatization of collective enterprises, and China's decision to enter the World Trade Organization (WTO), to name just a few prominent examples. The central driver of China's economic progress over the past twenty years has been the government's progressive withdrawal from direct management of the economy.[19] With the state sector shrinking dramatically, the economic center of gravity has shifted to the private sector through privatization, new ventures, and foreign-funded enterprises.

In 2001 the Chinese Communist Party shifted again as party secretary Jiang urged the party to recruit businesspeople as members and declared a "three represents" doctrine that stated the Party must represent capitalists in addition to workers and peasants.[20] China's transition to a socialist market economy appears set to continue going forward.

Road Map of the Book

This book has two primary objectives—to introduce Western readers to a sample of China's trailblazing entrepreneurs and companies, and to use their stories to illustrate more general principles that anyone can use to manage more effectively in unpredictable markets. The chapters that follow begin with the history of one entrepreneur and then generalize this specific story by laying out a general principle for managing uncertainty, including tools and techniques that entrepreneurs and executives can use in their own companies.

Chapter 2: Acknowledge the Fog of the Future

Managers must rethink their view of time in order to compete effectively in unpredictable markets like China. They must abandon the illusion that the future stretches out before them and that they can peer over the horizon, predict the future, and plan with accuracy and certainty. Instead, managers should adopt an unfolding view of time in which a steady stream of unanticipated threats and opportunities emerge, termed the *fog of the future* view of time. A constant flow of modest threats and opportunities is interspersed with periodic sudden-death threats that endanger a firm's very survival and golden opportunities during which a firm can create significant value in a short period of time. The brief history of Chinese Internet portal Sina illustrates this chapter's key themes.

Chapter 3: Conduct Reconnaissance into the Future

Surviving and thriving in unpredictable markets requires entrepreneurs and managers to develop a comprehensive awareness of the shifting situation and take systematic steps to anticipate possible threats and opportunities. Managers can improve their odds of succeeding by conducting reconnaissance into the future rather than relying on a preconceived plan. Managers can take several concrete steps to conduct reconnaissance into the future, including immersing themselves in the situation, keeping their mental map fluid, trusting their gut (after digesting plenty of data), incorporating multiple perspectives, and designing and conducting experiments. We illustrate reconnaissance into the future with the story of Ting Hsin's rise from humble origins to its status as one of the leading food groups in China.

Chapter 4: Outcycle the Competition

Simply sensing and anticipating emerging opportunities and threats is not enough. Executives must also translate their insight into effective action. But how can they do this? In this chapter we discuss how companies can move beyond insight to action by deploying the *SAPE cycle*, named after its four steps—sense, anticipate, prioritize, and execute. In unpredictable markets, companies compete in cycling through the SAPE cycle faster and more effectively than their rivals. This chapter describes the SAPE cycle as a whole, contrasts it with the strategic planning processes common in many established companies, and explains why it is well suited to competition in rapidly changing environments. We illustrate the SAPE cycle by analyzing how Legend overtook former personal computer leader Great Wall.

Chapter 5: Develop a Flexible Hierarchy

The term *flexible hierarchy* describes an organizational form that balances top-down priority setting with decentralized execution. In this chapter we describe how a flexible hierarchy functions and the steps necessary to develop it. We also provide suggestions on maintaining a sense of urgency even after a company has achieved significant success. We illustrate flexible hierarchy with the story of Chinese home appliance leader Haier.

Chapter 6: Manage Relationships Dynamically

This chapter argues that partnerships are necessary in order to share risk and obtain resources for succeeding in an unpredictable environment. The costs and benefits of partnerships, however, shift constantly, and entrepreneurs and executives must actively manage their dynamics. We identify a series of concrete actions to manage the dynamics of relationships over time. The rise of Galanz to national, and then global, leadership in the microwave oven industry illustrates the advantages of actively managing dynamic relationships.

Chapter 7: Go for the Gold

Unpredictable environments periodically throw out golden opportunities that allow firms to create significant value in a short period. These opportunities are fleeting, and in this chapter we introduce the *three windows of opportunity* framework to help managers and entrepreneurs systematically evaluate opportunities in order to recognize a golden opportunity when they see it and decide whether the timing is right to concentrate their resources to pursue the opportunity. Wahaha's rise to dominance in the beverage industry illustrates how companies can seize golden opportunities to establish market leadership.

Chapter 8: Get Big Right

This chapter discusses how to get big right, or scale a business effectively when pursuing a golden opportunity. The rapid growth required to seize a golden opportunity before one's rivals places enormous strains on a company's resources. Entrepreneurs may face big-company problems for the first time, for example, or struggle to raise the money required to fund growth. Successfully seizing a golden opportunity requires companies to overcome the myriad challenges inherent in rapid growth. This chapter discusses how entrepreneurs and managers can think more systematically about the challenges of scaling their organization, and illustrates these insights with examples from UTStarcom.

Chapter 9: Leading in an Unpredictable World

We conclude the book with some thoughts on the role of leadership in an unpredictable world, drawing heavily on insights from the entrepreneurs we studied.

Appendix: Research Design and Methodology

The appendix describes how we selected our industries and companies, gathered and analyzed data, and validated our findings.

Acknowledge the Fog of the Future

EXECUTIVES raised in stable contexts often flounder when plunged into the dynamism of the Chinese market. Chinese bureaucrats who ran state-owned enterprises under tight central planning, for example, have struggled to adapt to the rigors of a market economy. So too have Western managers who cut their teeth in Western Europe, Japan, or North America. Chinese bureaucrats and Western managers have struggled, in part, because they relied on a view of time ill-suited to China's dynamic market. They believed they could gaze deep into the future and, based on their predictions, develop long-term plans, methodically implement these strategies, and subsequently sustain their competitive advantage. Like captains of a ship in clear weather, they believed they could peer through a telescope into the distant horizon and set a clear course for the future.

Visibility into the future, however, was limited in China by uncertainty arising from rapid integration into global markets, rapidly shifting regulations at multiple levels of government, uneven evolution of

property rights, sporadic access to financing, and continuous technological change. The uncertainty of these individual variables as well
as interactions among them created a *fog of the future* that obscured
managers' foresight. Rather than ship captains peering through a telescope in clear weather, managers in China more closely resembled
race car drivers along an unfamiliar route in the fog. The successful
entrepreneurs we studied accepted their limited visibility into the future. Rather than relying on detailed long-term plans, these entrepreneurs focused on anticipating and seizing unforeseen opportunities,
responding to unexpected threats, constantly preparing for contingencies, and rapidly outmaneuvering other start-ups and resource-
rich multinationals. *Active waiting* is an approach to managing in
highly unpredictable markets that consists of anticipating and preparing for opportunities and threats that a manager can neither fully
predict nor control.

We use the story of Sina Corporation to illustrate the fog of the
future and active waiting.[1] With 2003 revenues of $114 million and
net profits of $31 million, Sina hosts China's leading Internet portal,
which was ranked the country's most popular online destination in
2003.[2] Sina translated its traffic into leadership among online advertisers and led China's portals in providing value-added services
such as news and horoscopes as short message services over mobile
phones. At year-end 2003, China's 80 million Internet users represented the second-largest market in the world, and some analysts
expected the country to overtake the United States in Internet users
by 2008.[3] Sina also targeted Chinese speakers globally with its
Mandarin-language Web sites serving mainland China, Hong Kong,
Taiwan, and North America. Many users consider Sina the most reliable source of online news in Chinese.

The company's history is itself as fascinating as any of the news
stories it reports. The company serves as an excellent case to illustrate how the interaction of multiple uncertain variables creates a fog
of the future. Sina's story combines the unpredictability of China's
economy with the roller-coaster history of dot-coms—companies
founded in the 1990s to seize opportunities created by the global rise
of the Internet. The Sina story also introduces us to Zhidong Wang, a
legendary computer programmer and serial entrepreneur in China,

and provides a glimpse into the evolution of Beijing's Zhongguancun district, often referred to as China's Silicon Valley.

Zhidong Wang and the Origins of Sina

Before discussing the fog of the future in China's Internet market and Sina's approach of actively waiting, we first provide a bit of historical context. The following sections describe Zhidong Wang's early career and the founding of Beijing Stone Rich Sight Information Technology Company, the software company cofounded by Wang in 1993 that evolved into Sina six years later. This background will serve as the context for our later discussion on the fog of the future and active waiting.

Zhidong Wang's Early Career

In 1984, Zhidong Wang left his hometown of Humen in the Guangdong province (host to China's early Special Economic Zones) and entered the elite Beijing University, where he majored in radio engineering. Wang's parents were both school teachers of modest means, but they still managed to send him approximately $7 per month to cover his living expenses for his first two years. By his third year, he had to pay his own way and worked for a local start-up assembling personal computers.

For a technically minded student, entering Beijing University or rival Tsinghua University in the mid-1980s was the Chinese equivalent of entering Stanford to study engineering as the personal computer revolution was taking off. Beijing and Tsinghua Universities were at the center of the Zhongguancun region of Beijing, then emerging as the epicenter of the high-tech revolution in China. Zhongguancun comprises a section of Beijing's Haidian district, where some technology researchers founded quasi-private ventures in the early 1980s. At the beginning, most of them sold electronic products, so Zhongguancun earned the nickname "Electronics Street." Since May 1988, when the State Council approved the establishment of the Haidian Experimental Zone for the development of high and new technology,

Zhongguancun has evolved into a leading technology cluster in China.[4] During the 1980s and 1990s, the surrounding district attracted alumni of Beijing University, Tsinghua University, and the Chinese Academy of Sciences, who founded hundreds of computer start-ups. Between 1983 and 1986, such early information technology leaders as Stone (founded in 1984), Kehai (1983), Founder (1986), Great Wall (1986), and Legend (1984) were founded there.

As a student, Wang was passionate about computers and idolized Western high-tech pioneers Steve Jobs and Bill Gates. Many of his classmates opted to study in the States, but as graduation drew near, Wang decided to pursue his fortune closer to home. He worried that studying to pass the graduate school admission tests, extending his studies, and moving abroad would burn too much time while he was impatient to jump into the fray. He later recalled: "Zhongguancun was already known as China's Silicon Valley. Since one of my feet was already in China's Silicon Valley, I decided to plant both my feet in it. I worried about losing so much time by going abroad."

Jumping into Zhongguancun was not completely straightforward, even for someone with Wang's technical background. In China's planned economy, all college graduates enjoyed the status of government officials and therefore received guaranteed jobs. The downside, however, was that the allocated positions were largely driven by the government's plans rather than the students' preferences. When Wang graduated in 1988, he was assigned a job as a technician in a dairy factory in a suburb on the outskirts of Beijing. Wang secured a leave without pay from the farm so that he could find a position with one of the local computer start-ups, and took a job with a ten-person computer start-up. Working in a small shop exposed Wang to every aspect of the business, from calling on customers to assembling computers, but he quickly gravitated to programming, where he demonstrated a genius for quickly writing complex code.

Wang's talent came to the attention of the CEO of the Founder Group—a spin-off from Beijing University that had emerged as one of China's leading information technology companies. Founder's CEO, the legendary Xuan Wang, invited Wang to join as a programmer. Free to focus on software development, Zhidong Wang's programming genius blossomed. In his first year on the job, Wang completed the first functional Chinese-language interface for the Windows operating system and in his spare time wrote BDwin, a program that enabled users to input Chinese characters, save them in a database, and freely shift from simplified Chinese (used in the People's Republic of China) to complicated Chinese (used in Taiwan) and to English. Wang's superiors at Founder considered the BDwin software a distraction from their core business and showed little interest in promoting the new software. Wang quit the company in 1991, leaving the source code with his former employer.

In April 1992, Wang contributed source code he had written after leaving Founder, and a Beijing University classmate provided the capital to found Beijing Suntendy Electronics Information Research Institute. At that time, China lacked the legal framework for founding a truly private enterprise, so the partners incorporated the start-up as a collective enterprise. The venture was founded to commercialize Chinese Star, a Chinese-language platform that helps users to read and write Chinese in a Western text operating system. The software quickly achieved popularity among Chinese users and after many years remained one of the leading Chinese-language platforms on the market. Despite the software's success, Wang and his partner disagreed about the company's direction. Wang, who served as the deputy general manager and head of technology, wanted to build a leading software company, whereas his partner hoped to earn a windfall by speculating in Beijing's booming real estate market. In August 1993, Wang submitted his resignation, again leaving the rights to the source code with his former employer.

Beijing Stone Rich Sight Information Technology Company

After Wang's professional setbacks, colleagues, friends, and his wife questioned whether it was possible to grow a successful software company in China, or whether Wang should make the move to Silicon Valley to pursue his dreams. Although Wang hit a personal and professional low at this juncture, he remained committed to building a world-class software company in Zhongguancun to develop cutting-edge software, rather than relying on outdated versions of American software. Despite his setbacks, Wang reminded himself that information technology would continue to progress in interesting ways, that China was an enormous market, that Zhongguancun remained a hotbed of innovation, and that he had demonstrated his ability to program world-class software.

In 1993, Wang teamed up with another star programmer, Yuanchao Yan, who shared his vision of developing a universal Chinese-language platform that would enable computers using an English operating system to recognize Chinese characters. Wang and Yan approached several leading computer and software firms, including Great Wall, Founder, and Legend, but they all planned to develop similar platforms in-house and expressed no interest in a joint venture. Finally, the Stone Group agreed to fund a joint venture in exchange for an ownership stake. Based on their previous experiences, the cofounders insisted that Stone invest at least $646,000 in a joint venture with the autonomy to focus exclusively on Chinese software. Wang and Yan would receive an equity stake in exchange for contributing technology. Stone agreed to the terms, and in December 1993 the joint venture Beijing Stone Rich Sight Information Technology Company (BSRS) began operations in Beijing.

Wang and his team of programmers worked day and night to develop a Chinese application platform, named RichWin, which consisted of millions of lines of code. The resulting program was technically sophisticated, but initial sales were sluggish because users were baffled by the confusing array of functions. Under Wang's supervision, the BSRS engineers revised the software in response to customer feedback, and RichWin quickly emerged as the de facto standard of Chinese-language application software. The company booked revenues of $430,000 in 1996 and more than doubled revenues in each of the following two years.[5]

From Wild Grass to Tall Tree

Although software sales were growing at a brisk pace, Wang worried that BSRS would be unable to sustain its early success. He observed that the Zhongguancun region produced "much wild grass, but few tall trees," meaning that many of the district's start-ups initially sprouted very rapidly but failed to scale. Wang also anticipated the day when established Western software companies such as Microsoft would train their sights on the Chinese market. In 1995, Wang visited Silicon Valley to seek out experienced investors who could help BSRS make the transition from wild grass to a tree tall enough to withstand the entry of foreign rivals. Wang engaged the San Francisco investment banking firm Robertson Stephens and received some very difficult feedback. His advisors worried that funding from the Stone Group might lead to conflicts of interest as BSRS grew, and questioned the management structure, which included Wang's brother overseeing source code and his wife administering the finances. His advisors recommended that he hire professional managers for key positions and seek out venture capitalists to fund and help grow the company. Wang initially resisted these recommendations but ultimately adopted them.

Wang's advisors also urged him to evaluate the Internet as a potential once-in-a-lifetime opportunity. During his first trip to Silicon Valley, Wang discovered the Internet; he stayed online for three days and nights, surfing and downloading software. Although Wang quickly grasped the Internet's potential, he was reluctant to change course suddenly from BSRS's software focus. On the other hand, he did not want to miss the window of opportunity opened by the Internet. In May 1996, Wang launched SRSnet.com, a Web site that offered mainland users Chinese-language news as well as online community services. Many employees derided Wang's top-down Internet initiative as his toy, but the site's success allowed BSRS to win the contract to develop the Chinese government's Internet application software in early 1997.

BSRS's beachhead on the Internet attracted the attention of Daniel Mao, a Stanford-educated venture capitalist with San Francisco–based Walden International. Mao was impressed by the software development capabilities at BSRS and Wang's toehold in the Internet, and Walden led a syndicate of investors that injected $6.5 million in BSRS to fund the company's online expansion. The company's Web site was moderately successful, but the breakout occurred in 1998, when its real-time and in-depth coverage of the World Cup competition attracted widespread attention in China. The company solidified its early lead by forging relationships with a host of news providers. When North American Treaty Organization forces accidentally bombed China's embassy in Yugoslavia in May 1999, the company's Web site reported the event before China's official news media.

Mao introduced Wang to dozens of Internet companies in Silicon Valley to seek a potential partner. While making these rounds, Wang met Daniel Chiang, the cofounder and CEO of Hua Yuan, a company based in Cupertino, California, that hosted the Sinanet.com portal (the company was frequently referred to as Sinanet.com based on the success of its portal). The portal offered Chinese-language content to users in the United States and Taiwan. Chiang was a cofounder of Trend Micro and had led that company through a successful initial public offering and achieved a market capitalization that exceeded $1 billion. Chiang left Trend Micro to establish Sinanet.com to seize the opportunity presented by the Internet. In 1999, BSRS joined forces with Sinanet.com, and the merged entity was renamed Sina Corporation (Sina). Later that year, Sina launched a Web site targeting the Hong Kong market. Sina's Chinese, U.S., Taiwanese, and Hong Kong Web sites helped it achieve its objective of "uniting all people of Chinese heritage in online communities with the highest quality information." In 1999, two independent surveys ranked Sina.com as China's top Internet site.

In late 1999, the company raised $60 million in financing from investors, including Dell Computer, Softbank, and Pacific Century Cyberworks. In April 2000, Sina beat Chinese portal rivals Sohu.com and NetEase in offering its stock on America's NASDAQ stock exchange and raised an additional $68 million. The following month, the stock jumped from its initial price of $17 to over $54 per share, a level that valued the company's equity at $2 billion. The company's valuation was driven by expectations that its revenues from online advertising would continue to rise explosively, with some equity analysts predicting annual advertising revenues in excess of $100 million by 2004.[6] The company's revenues from online advertising increased twentyfold, from approximately $0.5 million in fiscal year 1999 to over $11 million the following year.

The party quickly ended, however. By late 2000, analysts were predicting a massive shakeout of Chinese dot-coms after the sudden collapse of Hong Kong–based Chinese Books Cyberstore, a company that had aspired to be Asia's Amazon.com. By that time, Sina had accumulated an operating loss of nearly $100 million in two years. Worse yet, advertising revenues stalled and then declined between 2001 and 2002. Sina's share price hovered at just over $1 through much of the autumn, a dangerous place to be because the NASDAQ de-listed stocks that consistently traded at less than $1 per share.

In June 2001, Sina's directors replaced Wang with Daniel Mao, who had served on the board since 1997. Mao took dramatic actions to stop the bleeding, reducing the company's sales and marketing expenses by 43 percent and cutting product development outlays by nearly one-third. These actions decreased the company's losses by half and preserved Sina's cash stockpile of nearly $100 million, which bought Mao time to wait for the next big opportunity.

Mao and his colleagues used this time well. They didn't wait passively, but designed and ran experiments to explore various pathways to increase revenues, including fee-based premium services such as expanded e-mail, short messaging services (SMS), and online games. The company created a division to help companies and government agencies design and implement their online systems, such as corporate e-mail and online publishing. In September 2001, Sina entered into an alliance with Hong Kong–based Sun Television to syndicate Sun's television programs and explore options to expand content distribution. Not all of Sina's experiments paid off, of course. Commentators derided the Sun Television deal, for example, as a desperate ploy by two floundering companies.[7] Fee-based SMS on mobile phones, in contrast, proved to be a golden opportunity. From virtually nothing in 2001, Sina's SMS business grew to contribute the majority of the mobile value-added service revenues of nearly $64 million for calendar year 2003, which surpassed the $41 million revenue from online advertising during the same period. Online gaming in 2004 was also showing great promise as a future source of profits and revenues. The incremental sales allowed Sina to earn its first operating profit and drove its stock price over $30 per share.

Sina's brief history has been a roller coaster with great highs and plummeting lows, and the ride is likely to be exciting going forward as well. Most important, for our purposes, it illustrates some critical aspects of strategy in turbulent markets, which we discuss in more general terms in the remainder of the chapter.

Navigating the Fog of the Future

After jumping into the Internet fray, Sina faced a very unpredictable future. As part of the company's initial public offering on the NAS-DAQ market, Sina managers identified some of the variables that could influence its future performance. The list in table 2-1 underscores the level of unpredictability facing Sina's executives. Unpredictability occurs in contexts that are *complex* (i.e., multiple factors influence firms' performance), *dynamic* (i.e., many of these variables are individually uncertain and volatile), and *interactive* (i.e., variables can interact with one another to create unexpected outcomes).[8] Taken as a whole, these variables sharply reduced Sina executives' visibility into the future.

Drawing on the language of military theory, we use the term *fog of the future* to describe the unpredictability inherent in complex, dynamic, and interactive markets such as the Internet in China. The military thinker Karl von Clausewitz used the imagery of fog to evoke the unpredictability inherent in military conflict.[9] In combat, military leaders must contend with unexpected attacks, the enemy's deliberate deception, misinterpreted communication, ambushes, abrupt changes in weather, breakdowns in logistics, friendly fire from allies, unexpectedly strong resistance, miscommunication among divisions, equipment failure, abrupt changes in orders from headquarters, and a thousand other variables that confound even the most thorough leader's strategy. The disorder, uncertainty, and fluidity of battle can also work in their favor, however, and provide opportunities to seize the initiative. Managers in unpredictable markets proceed into the future much like an army advancing into unfamiliar terrain, and the fog of the future describes the limited visibility that is a fact of life for managers in these contexts. Many people assert that the world is growing more unpredictable, but the fog of the future has always been and always will be a fact of life in business (see the box entitled "Same As It Ever Was").

TABLE 2-1

Sina's unpredictable future in 2000

Operating risks

Limited operating history makes it difficult to ensure internal or external targets
will be met
Unproven business model puts revenues at risk
Ability to build, retain, and manage relationships with content providers
Ability to attract and retain qualified management and employees
Potential fluctuations in exchange rates of Chinese, U.S., Taiwanese, and
Hong Kong currency
Access to funding when necessary for investment in growth or operations

Market risks

Acceptance of the Internet as an advertising medium compared with traditional
media
Ability to attract advertisers to Sina.com versus competitors
Ability to build sufficient network of users to attract advertisers
Reliable means of verifying effectiveness of online advertising
Dependence on a small number of advertisers that can cancel contracts on
short notice
Increasing awareness of Sina.com brand and customer loyalty
Customers' concerns about security, reliability, and cost of Internet
Development of means of payment by customers inexperienced with credit cards
Ability to introduce new offerings to attract new and retain existing users

Competitive risks

Competitive pressures from new entrants in market with low barriers to entry
Entry into China of large, well-capitalized companies such as Microsoft, Yahoo!,
and AOL, among others
Downward pressure on online advertising prices
Inability to match competitors' new product and service offerings in a timely fashion

Technology risks

Sina.com's ability to upgrade technology to support increased traffic and
expanded services
Continued development of telecommunications infrastructure by ChinaNet,
China's government-owned network
Lack of access to alternative networks in case of disruption of ChinaNet
Potential need to register encryption software with Chinese authorities and
develop new software

Legal and regulatory risks

Potential content restrictions and regulations by Chinese government agencies
Lack of clarity about the legality of current and future foreign investment in the
Internet sector
Risks surrounding organizational structure separating out Chinese subsidiary to
circumvent restrictions on foreign direct investment
Access to approval for foreign exchange
Uncertain legal environment surrounding privacy, pricing, content, copyrights,
antitrust, etc.
Inability to protect intellectual property within Chinese legal system

Source: Company documents and author's analysis.

Same As It Ever Was

IS THE WORLD becoming more unpredictable? The fog of the future is clearly a fact of life in many markets, including the so-called BRIC economies (Brazil, Russia, India, and China) and technology-intensive industries such as information technology, telecommunications, and medical devices. Many prominent strategy and management thinkers have asserted that the global economy is experiencing a general shift toward greater volatility. Many individual managers echo these assertions and believe that their own industries have grown less predictable in recent years.

The evidence of increasing unpredictability, however, is far from conclusive. Statistical analyses of large samples of companies have revealed mixed results.[10] Some studies find limited evidence that volatility has increased across a range of industries, whereas others have found more uncertainty only among certain sectors or over brief time periods. Other studies have failed to unearth any evidence of greater volatility whatsoever. Indeed, the Austrian economist Joseph Schumpeter coined the memorable phrase "creative destruction" not in the 1990s but in the 1940s, suggesting that unpredictable markets have always been with us. Similarly, management guru Peter Drucker has been describing the transition from a stable past to an uncertain future for decades.

Based on the evidence, we come to a simple yet controversial position: managers have always faced the fog of the future, and they always will. In fact, the essence of management is effective action in an unpredictable world. Of course, economies have enjoyed periods of relative stability, such as the decades of the planned economy in China and the United States' boom years between 1950 and 1970. These pauses in the action, however, represent the exception rather than the rule of economic development throughout history. Moreover, some industries, such as China's Internet sector, are simply messier than others. But these are differences of degree, not kind.

If you assume that unpredictability is inherent in business, a different question arises: Why do so many theories assume the opposite? Much of current strategic theory assumes that markets tend to a stable equilibrium, that managers can foresee the future with considerable accuracy, and that firms can sustain their positions into the indefinite future. Why do the theories that exaggerate our predictive ability enjoy such wide currency?

Management ideas, like any other product, have a supply side and a demand side. On the supply side lie management academics and consultants. Much of the influential thinking in strategy emerged from research conducted in the United States in the decades following World War II, a relatively stable time in the history of the global economy. This period of industrial stability coincided with the rise of economics' influence on corporate strategy. By assuming away uncertainty or limiting its scope (e.g., to competitors' moves in game theory), economists created tractable models that could be solved mathematically.

On the demand side, business students and executives enthusiastically embraced models imbuing managers with a high level of predictive ability. Managers adopted models that downplayed the role of unpredictability because these theories increased their sense of control. A belief in a predictable future and sustainable competitive advantages infused managers with the confidence to act, but this sense of control over the future is illusory in many sectors of the global economy, including China's dynamic market. Worse yet, assuming unwarranted visibility into the future is not even necessary. Throughout history, entrepreneurs have acted decisively and effectively despite unpredictability. In fact, managers can march more effectively into the fog of the future when they acknowledge their inability to predict the future. This chapter, and indeed the entire book, provide practical principles for acting in the face of uncertainty.

When advancing into the fog of the future, managers must abandon the assumptions that they can forecast with clarity and certainty, draft a detailed long-term plan, implement a strategy at their leisure, and sustain their competitive advantage. Rather, they must accept their limited visibility into what is to come. Competing in an unpredictable environment is very disorienting, particularly to managers accustomed to more stable contexts. Viewed conceptually, however, the fog of the future has two clear implications. First, the steady stream of unexpected changes creates opportunities for nimble competitors to seize. Second, these changes threaten established firms' sources of competitive advantage, and in some cases their very survival.

The fog of the future is depicted graphically in figure 2-1. In this figure, the vertical axis pointing upward measures the magnitude of opportunity for new value creation enabled by an external event, and the downward-pointing axis represents the magnitude of threat an event poses to an established company's market position, resources, or competencies. The lines of the graph represent these magnitudes over time, much as the lines of a seismograph would measure the intensity of earthquakes. Magnitude in this graph, however, is not a

FIGURE 2-1

Fog of the future

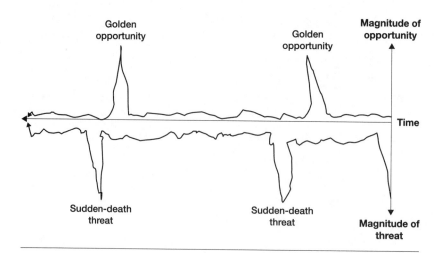

measure of an event's importance in some abstract sense, but rather a specific measure of an event's impact on the firm's opportunities for new value creation or threats to existing competitive advantage. Thus, it is quite possible that a major world event, such as a war or change in political party, would not register as a large shift, whereas industry-specific changes such as technological innovations could loom large for a firm.

The most important aspect of this diagram is that the lines are records of historical events, not predictions of future events. Like a seismograph, these lines register the past rather than forecast the future. In unpredictable markets, managers know that threats and opportunities are possible, but cannot forecast their specific form, timing, or magnitude with precision. When Wang began his career in Zhongguancun in 1988, for example, he could not envision the opportunities offered by the Internet, nor could he foresee that some-day his business might be threatened by the entry of companies such as Yahoo!, which didn't even exist at the time. Of course, he would have known in some general sense that the future held opportunities and threats, but without knowing their specific form he could not plan into the distant future to seize those opportunities and guard against those threats. The fog of the future highlights the fundamen-tal challenge of management—effective action in the face of an un-predictable future. This view also contrasts with notions of time implicit in established strategy theory (see the box entitled "Fortress View of Time").

Golden Opportunities

The good news about unpredictable markets is that they create new opportunities. We define an opportunity as a novel combination of resources that fills an unmet market need and creates value in excess of the cost to acquire the use of necessary resources.[11] Opportunities resemble new dishes that combine ingredients (i.e., resources) using new recipes (i.e., novel combinations) to meet diners' tastes (i.e., unmet market needs). The culinary analogy not only illustrates the essence of an opportunity but also clarifies the sources of new opportunities.

Fortress View of Time

TO UNDERSTAND what is different about the fog of the future, let's begin with a quick overview of strategic thinking.[12] The purpose of any business, according to strategic theory, is threefold: to *create* value, to *capture* it, and to *sustain* it into the future. Firms create value by producing goods or services that are worth more than the cost of necessary inputs. This value can be distributed in any number of ways, of course—to customers in the form of lower prices, for example, or as taxes paid to the government. Business strategy theory, however, focuses on how firms capture (or, in technical terms, "appropriate") the value they create. Finally, prevailing models of business strategy posit that companies create value by building a competitive advantage that differentiates them from their competitors, thereby allowing them to sustain their value creation and capturing into the future.

Prevailing views of strategy recommend that executives first identify an attractive market that will provide high profits in the future because barriers to entry—such as government regulation or economies of scale—keep rivals at bay.[13] Managers then erect defenses to fortify their position. Ideally, these defenses also protect against customers or suppliers exerting too much power and eroding profits. To return to military imagery, this approach resembles finding a high hill (i.e., the attractive market position) and fortifying it with barbed wire and machine gun turrets to defend the stronghold from attacks on all sides. Executives can secure their position by building valuable resources or competencies.[14] Resources are assets that a company controls, which can be tangible (e.g., specialized factories, prime real estate) or intangible (e.g., a well-known brand, a good relationship with the local government, patented technology, or an established distribution channel). Competencies, in contrast, refer not to what a company *owns,* but to what it *does well*.[15] This view of strategy implicitly assumes a view of time in which entrepreneurs and managers can gaze deep into the future and identify a position that will be attractive for years (or decades) to come. Based on their foresight, they develop a plan to build the resources or develop the competencies needed to protect their position.[16] Next they methodically build those resources and competencies. Their details of the plan, of course, evolve over time but follow the broad trajectory laid out initially. Once they have staked out a position and fortified it, managers subsequently focus on sustaining their position into the indefinite future. (Figure 2-2 depicts this process graphically.)

Although many people take this view of time for granted, it actually is built on some very strong (and questionable) assumptions.[17] First, the fortress view of time assumes that managers can predict the future with sufficient accuracy to decide which position or resources will be valuable in the future. The longer the period required to develop resources or competencies, the more important the role of foresight. The fortress view also assumes that once an attractive position is staked out and valuable resources or competencies established, they can be sustained into the future. The notion of sustainability implies that the best way to predict the future is by extrapolating from the present.[18] This framework, of course, assumes that competitive rivalry and substitution erode value over time, but that even this is gradual and predictable. Discontinuous changes are modeled as extremely rare events preceded and followed by long periods of equilibrium.[19]

The fortress view of time, which extrapolates the known present into the future, is so intuitive that it's often hard to imagine other conceptions of time. Time can, however, be modeled in many ways, including steady passage (e.g., a clock ticking), recurrent cycles (e.g., seasons of the year), or life cycles passing through clearly delineated stages (e.g., people progressing through youth, adolescence, maturity, and decline).[20] The fog of the future presents a useful alternative to the planning view of time that helps entrepreneurs and managers survive and thrive in complex, dynamic, and interactive markets.

FIGURE 2-2

Fortress view of time

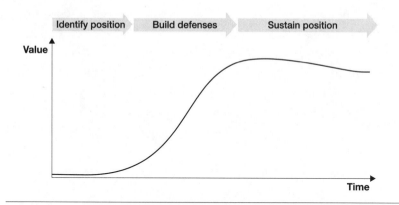

New dishes emerge in one of three ways. First, a shift in tastes creates new demands. The popularity of the low-carbohydrate Atkins diet, for example, spurred a craving among its adherents for recipes including low-carb pasta. Second, new dishes emerge when new ingredients appear on the scene. The introduction of the tomato to Europe in the sixteenth century, for example, spurred a revolution in Italian cuisine. Finally, new dishes emerge when a creative spark engenders a novel combination of existing resources to meet an existing hunger. The English Earl of Sandwich, for example, is credited with combining bread and meat into the dish that bears his name so he could eat without interrupting his gambling. Bread, meat, and gambling had all been around for millennia, but Sandwich gets the recognition for combining the first two in a way that would allow him to get more of the third.

Like new dishes, new business opportunities similarly arise due to changes in customer preferences, the availability of new resources, and novel combinations of existing resources. The good news about dynamic markets such as China is that the shifts in the broader context that limit predictability also spur new customer preferences and make available new resources that create opportunities. China's transition to a market economy and opening to the West dramatically reduced predictability compared with the era of state planning; however, these changes in the broader context also increased consumers' disposable income and level of technical sophistication, and provided entrepreneurs such as Wang access to previously unobtainable resources, including foreign funds, Western technology, and the expertise and contacts of venture capitalists such as Mao. Table 2-2 summarizes some sources of new opportunities.

Not all opportunities are created equal. Companies in rapidly changing markets such as China face a steady stream of small and medium-sized opportunities, interspersed with periodic chances to create significant value. The pattern of frequent small changes interspersed with periodic large ones is not limited to business environments, and research on dynamic systems has found that the frequency of changes is inversely related to their magnitude across a variety of complex systems.[21] We use the term *golden opportunity* to describe the infrequent occasions when a firm can create significant value in a short period of time. Recall that Wang founded BSRS as a software company—and, of course, faced many chances to grow revenues by selling software. The defining moment in the company's history came, however, when Wang, under the guidance of his advisors, seized the unexpected opportunity arising with the Internet. Subsequently, Sina pursued many small and medium-sized opportunities, but short messaging services proved golden for the company.

TABLE 2-2

Sources and examples of new opportunities

New customer needs

Macroeconomic changes
- Low interest rates spur new housing demand

Demographic trends
- Aging population increases demand for pensions

Changes in consumer preferences
- Health consciousness increases demand for nutritional supplements and bottled water

Regulatory shifts
- Move from planned to market economy increases disposable income and demand for new products

New resources available

New technology
- Internet and mobile telephony enable new services

Privatization frees resources
- Chinese government sells stakes in formerly state-owned enterprises

Globalization of resource markets
- Outsourcing of production to China

New combinations of existing resources

New business model
- Southwest Airlines

Process innovations
- Supply-chain improvements

A golden opportunity arises when a confluence of circumstances allows a company to have a large impact on its market with relatively limited resources. The distinction between force and impact helps illustrate this point. *Force* refers to the amount of energy exerted, whereas *impact* describes the effect of applied energy on another body. The impact resulting from a given level of force exerted can differ. The same force, for example, applied in a series of small taps will have less impact than a single blow delivered at the right place at one point in time. To cite another example, a small poke when someone is off balance can topple a person, whereas it would have no impact if the person had his or her footing. A golden opportunity can be visualized as a period of time when the external context allows a deployment of resources to have a disproportionate market impact. BSRS was able to have a significant impact because it invested resources just as the Internet market was poised to take off and before any competitor had entrenched itself as a market leader. The same resources invested before the market was ready or after a leader had emerged would have had little impact. (Chapter 7, "Go for the Gold," discusses the circumstances that are conducive to making a major impact with limited resources.)

Sudden-Death Threats

Golden opportunities are the good news of turbulent markets like China, but sudden-death threats are the bad news. *Sudden-death threat* describes a major environmental shock that threatens a company's business with extinction. Threats, like opportunities, vary in intensity, with the periodic major hazard interspersed among many smaller nuisances. Sudden-death threats come in several varieties: threats can stimulate demand for substitute products (e.g., online travel sites versus travel agencies), reduce barriers to entry (e.g., China opening its domestic banking industry to foreign competitors), or diminish the value of resources by changing the context in which those resources are employed (e.g., the entry of low-cost, point-to-point rivals reduced the value of established carriers' hubs and large planes).[22]

Like golden opportunities, sudden-death threats generally arise from changes in the broader context outside the entrepreneur's control. Consider the fate of InfoHighway, the early leader in China's Internet space. In early 1996, a large billboard in Zhongguancun asked, "How far is China away from the Internet?" The answer— 1,500 meters—referred to the distance from the sign to InfoHighway's headquarters building. Equating InfoHighway and China's access to the Internet was a reasonable claim in 1996, when the company was the best-known online brand in the country and looked likely to lead China's Internet market. Like Sina, InfoHighway was founded by a charismatic technologist: Shuxin Zhang graduated in 1986 from the prestigious University of Science and Technology of China (USTC), where she served as the student president in the predominantly male institution. She discovered the Internet on a trip to the United States in 1994 (a year before Wang) and founded Info-Highway that same year as an Internet service provider. Modeled after America Online, InfoHighway allowed Chinese subscribers to connect to the Internet with dial-up modems to access news content, chat rooms, and even some overseas Web sites. In 1996, Zhang raised close to $6 million in funding from the XingFa group, a state-owned conglomerate with deep pockets (again, a year before Wang raised a similar sum), and the next year entered into an alliance with Microsoft.

InfoHighway faced a threat to its business model as an Internet service provider in June 1997 when the Ministry of Post and Telecommunications (MPT) announced an investment of nearly $850 million in the "169" network intended to broaden China's access to the Internet. The new network competed head-on with InfoHighway, offered much lower access fees to stimulate adoption of the new technology, and was backed by a state-run ministry with deep pockets and a monopoly on telecommunications regulation. There had been indications that the Internet service provider business model might be in danger in China since at least 1996, not only because of possible entry by the MPT, but also because Yahoo!'s initial public offering in April of that year suggested that portals were the wave of the future. Whereas other early leaders like Sohu.com shifted their business model from providing Internet services to hosting a portal beginning in 1996, InfoHighway was slow to respond to the sudden-death threat, with disastrous consequences. By 1999, InfoHighway had lost its initial lead and dropped out of China's top ten Internet brands. The next year, it plummeted to number 131, and soon thereafter existed only as a memory.

Active Waiting

Perhaps the most important implication of the fog of the future is that managers and entrepreneurs cannot impose their will on the future in markets that are complex, dynamic, and interactive. They cannot conjure up a golden opportunity just because their existing business is declining. They cannot make golden opportunities appear on a regular quarterly basis because their shareholders demand predictable increases in revenues and profits. They cannot delay a sudden-death threat because their company is ill-prepared to weather the storm. What, then, can entrepreneurs and managers do to navigate the fog of the future? Opportunity is often defined as the meeting of preparation and favorable circumstances, whereas disaster results from the collision of an unprepared company and an unforeseen threat. The differences between the successful and less successful entrepreneurs we studied in our research had as much to do with what they did in the periods of relative calm as what they did when faced with sudden-death threats or golden opportunities.

We end this chapter with the notion of *active waiting*, which consists of anticipating, preparing for, and quickly seizing opportunities and dealing with threats whose form, magnitude, or timing can neither be predicted nor controlled. Active waiting has several components, which we will elaborate throughout the rest of this book, including conducting reconnaissance into the future to anticipate emerging threats and opportunities (chapter 3); building a war chest of financial and human resources that can be deployed against multiple contingencies (chapters 5 and 7); establishing the processes and organization to quickly seize opportunities and respond to threats (chapters 4 through 8); and adopting the leadership style appropriate for an unpredictable world (chapter 9). For now, let it suffice to say that in an unpredictable world, managers must recognize that a critical part of their job consists of actively waiting for sudden-death threats and golden opportunities that are largely beyond their ability to forecast or control and yet that remain critical to their success and survival.

Summary

When navigating the fog of the future, entrepreneurs and managers must abandon the fortress view of time and accept the unpredictability inherent in complex, dynamic, and interactive markets. Active waiting is an approach for surviving and thriving in an unpredictable world. This chapter's key lessons are summarized in the following list. The next chapter describes how to conduct reconnaissance into an unpredictable future and illustrates its points with the story of Ting Hsin, the leader in China's instant noodle market.

- *Fog of the future* refers to the unpredictability inherent in markets that are complex (i.e., multiple factors influence a firm's performance), dynamic (i.e., many of these variables are individually uncertain and volatile), and interactive (i.e., variables interact with one another to create unexpected outcomes). The term *fog of the future* underscores managers' limited visibility into the future.

- The *fortress view of time* underlies the dominant models of business strategy. According to this view, managers can gaze deep into the future, identify an industry position that will be attractive for years to come, systematically build the resources and competencies to fortify the position, and then sustain their advantage into the indefinite future. This view assumes that managers can foresee the future with accuracy and certainty and that once a position has been fortified, it can and should be sustained into the future.

- A *golden opportunity* refers to an occasion when a firm can create significant value in a short period of time. New opportunities result from new customer preferences, newly available resources, and novel combinations of existing resources. Shifts in the broader context create new preferences and free resources, which in turn create new opportunities.

- *Sudden-death threats* are major environmental shocks that threaten an established company's business with extinction. Sudden-death threats differ from more frequent hazards in their magnitude, and challenge a firm's ability to create, capture, and sustain value.

- *Active waiting* consists of anticipating and preparing for opportunities and threats that a manager can neither fully predict nor control.

THREE

Conduct Reconnaissance into the Future

T HE LAST CHAPTER argued that entrepreneurs and managers must shift their view of time to compete effectively in unpredictable markets. They must abandon their comfortable belief that they can peer deep into the future and instead adopt an unfolding view of time in which modest opportunities and threats emerge in a steady stream interspersed with periodic golden opportunities and sudden-death threats. Corporate success in unpredictable environments results in large part from firms' ability to anticipate major shocks and respond to them more effectively and quickly than their rivals.

But how can managers effectively navigate in such an unpredictable world? This chapter argues that managers should conduct *reconnaissance into the future*. Reconnaissance into the future describes the process of surveying a complex and volatile environment and forming a mental map of the emerging situation to better anticipate emerging threats and opportunities. Entrepreneurs or managers competing in a rapidly changing market should act based on this map of the emerging situation, rather than relying on a preconceived plan, especially one formulated by staff at a distant headquarters. We illustrate the benefits of reconnaissance into the future using the story of Ting Hsin, one of China's leading food companies, and close the chapter with some concrete steps managers and entrepreneurs can take to conduct effective reconnaissance in their own businesses.

Ting Hsin and the Rise of the Master Kong Brand

By 2004, Ting Hsin had already made significant progress toward achieving its vision of becoming the leading food group in greater China.[1] Tingyi—the group's publicly listed subsidiary that traded on the Hong Kong stock exchange—booked 2003 revenues of $1.3 billion and had an enterprise value of $1.9 billion.[2] The Tianjin-based Tingyi controlled Master Kong (one of the best-recognized consumer brands in China) and an extensive distribution network that included 344 sales offices serving nearly five thousand wholesalers and fifty thousand retailers throughout the People's Republic of China. At the end of 2003, Tingyi was the leader in China's market for instant noodles, with a 44 percent share of market by value; ready-to-drink tea, with 47 percent market share; and sandwich crackers, with nearly one-quarter of the market. In addition to its stake in Tingyi, the Ting Hsin Group also controlled Wei Chuan (Taiwan's second-largest food company) as well as Hymart (a chain of hypermarket and shopping malls in China), Buynow (a large personal computer retailer in Beijing), and DICOS (a fast-food chain with over two hundred stores in China).

The Humble Origins of the Ting Hsin Group

Ting Hsin's market leadership is impressive by any standards, but particularly in light of the group's late entry into China's food market—Ting Hsin sold its first package of instant noodles in August 1992. Nor was the foray into Chinese packaged food made from a position of strength, but rather as a last-ditch effort to gain traction in the mainland's booming market by four brothers originally from Taiwan. Ting Hsin traces its origins to the Ting Hsin Oil Plant, founded by Hede Wei in rural Changhua, Taiwan, in 1958. Changhua, located in west-central Taiwan, is known as "the granary of Taiwan." Hede Wei's small workshop processed cooking oil, and his three daughters and four sons joined the family business immediately after completing high school. Each of the Wei children had a specific job, ranging from tending the oil pot to supervising successive pressings of seeds to extract oil. Hede Wei was a strict and frugal manager. The children later recalled that if one of them passed an oil seed on the ground without picking it up, their father would tweak their ear with his finger as punishment for their carelessness.

When Hede Wei died of a heart attack in 1978, the children were shocked to learn that the oil plant's liabilities of $317,000 equaled its assets, leaving them no capital to build the business. "We had to start from zero," oldest brother Ing-Chou later recalled. Despite their limited resources, the four brothers decided to continue the food oil business in Taiwan. Their opportunities for growth, however, were limited because Taiwan's cooking oil business was mature, and small players like Ting Hsin faced entrenched market leaders. Facing limited prospects in Taiwan, the four Wei brothers turned their attention to the mainland. In the words of Ying-Chiao, the second-oldest brother, "When we took over the business from father, Uni-President was already the number one food company in Taiwan, but in mainland China, it was still a level playing field. Whether you were a big or small player, everyone began at the same starting line."

Third Try Is a Charm

Ting Hsin's success on the mainland did not come easily or quickly. In 1988, with initial capital of $5.5 million raised from friends and relatives, the youngest Wei brother—Yin-Heng—left Taiwan to explore the mainland market. When the 28-year-old Yin-Heng arrived in Beijing, he noticed that many consumers were still using low-quality cooking oil; thus, he established a joint venture to produce the superior cooking oil common in Taiwan. The premium oil was launched under the Tinghao brand and was supported by an aggressive television advertising campaign. Tinghao oil, with its premium quality, was priced two to three times higher than that of government-subsidized cooking oil products in the market. Consumers recognized the oil's high quality and purchased it as an occasional gift. However, it was too expensive for most consumers to use on a daily basis, and sales were disappointing.

The lack of infrastructure in mainland China, moreover, required Ting Hsin to invest in operations to support the cooking oil business. The Wei brothers invested in a range of supporting businesses, including specialized trucks to transport the oil and dedicated carriers to maintain quality throughout the distribution chain. All these costs added up. To add insult to injury, local competitors leveraged support from local governments to secure access to low-cost raw materials. Burdened with high relative costs and lower than expected revenues, Ting Hsin exited the cooking oil business.

Not deterred by the setback, Yin-Heng found another business opportunity in producing and selling egg rolls. In 1991, Ting Hsin introduced Konglai branded egg rolls into the market from the company's production facility in the city of Jinan, capital of Shandong province. Tingyi used superior-quality raw materials and positioned its Konglai brand as a premium product relative to existing egg rolls. Ting Hsin conducted an aggressive advertising campaign in northern China touting its product's superior quality. As with cooking oil, however, actual demand failed to meet even the company's worst-case scenario. The company's advertising and high quality built awareness, but high prices again constrained consumer adoption. By the end of 1991, Yin-Heng had depleted nearly all funds earmarked for the mainland and had yet to establish a profitable business. That same year, the brothers established the Tianjin Tingyi International Food Company with the intent to produce biscuits in a last-ditch effort to gain traction on the mainland.

Then opportunity knocked unexpectedly. To save money, Yin-Heng traveled by train (in the least expensive class, which offered only uncomfortable hard seats) and packed his own meals. During an eighteen-hour train trip to Beijing, Yin-Heng opened a package of instant noodles that he had brought from Taiwan. The aromatic noodles attracted the attention of other passengers on the train. The youngest Wei brother shared the noodles with his fellow travelers, who devoured the flavorful noodles. Yin-Heng conducted some quick-and-dirty market research and discovered that China's instant noodle market was divided into two extremes. Many competitors sold low-end packaged noodles at rock-bottom prices. The Wei brothers learned that the first instant noodles were introduced into the Chinese market in the early 1970s; twenty years later, there were over 350 production lines of instant noodles in operation on the mainland. The producers churned out low-quality products in shabby packaging without investment in brand. At the other extreme were the high-end imported noodles like the ones that had attracted so much attention on the train. These were a luxury good, available at airports and boutiques but priced well beyond the reach of the average consumer.

Master Kong Conquers the Noodle Market

Historians dispute the origins of noodles, although some believe that Arab traders first used dried pasta as a means to preserve food during extended treks through the desert.[3] The Chinese have eaten noodles at least since the Han dynasty, over two thousand years ago—centuries before Marco Polo is reputed to have introduced them to Western cuisine after his journeys through China. In Chinese tradition, lengthy noodles symbolize long life and are often eaten at festive occasions to bring longevity. The first instant noodles were developed in Japan after World War II by Momofuku Ando, who introduced instant Ramen as a high-quality noodle that could be consumed anytime, anywhere. In 1958 Ando's company, Nissin Foods, introduced the first instant Ramen noodle, which could be removed from its plastic wrapping, placed in a bowl, covered with boiling water, and eaten three minutes later. Although Japanese food companies and retailers initially disparaged the product, consumers enthusiastically adopted it, and by the early 1970s instant noodles had made their way to most markets around the world, although the composition, thickness of noodle, and flavoring varied across regions.

Across China, for example, sweet foods were associated with the south, sour with the east, salty with the north, and spicy with the west (particularly Sichuan, or Szechuan, as it is sometimes translated).

The history of instant noodles would have been news to the Wei brothers, who had no experience whatsoever with that product. The brothers believed, however, that they had chanced upon a golden opportunity to provide a high-quality instant noodle at an affordable price for the mass market. Recognizing the differences in taste across regions, the Wei brothers conducted painstaking research to understand consumers' preferences. They carried out taste tests on tens of thousands of consumers and introduced successive refinements of the product based on earlier results.

Their research revealed that northern consumers in cities like Beijing and Tianjin preferred thick wheat noodles with a strong beef flavor. The brothers were also keen to incorporate the lessons from their earlier failures. Determined not to price the product beyond the average consumer's ability to pay, the Weis used their research to identify a sweet spot on pricing that was above the low-end noodles but well below the imported noodles. To reduce their fixed costs, the brothers converted the Tianjin factory from biscuit production to packaged noodle production and persuaded suppliers from Taiwan to bear the cost of providing supporting facilities and services rather than doing everything themselves.

In August 1992, Ting Hsin launched its first instant noodles under the Master Kong brand. The Wei brothers engaged marketing experts from Taiwan to help them position the Master Kong brand and created the logo of a cartoon chef with outstretched arms now ubiquitous in Chinese food stores. "Kong" in Chinese refers to healthiness, signaling the company's intent to provide healthy and nutritious products to Chinese consumers, and "Master" expressed respect and sincerity, which Ting Hsin used to signal its commitment to consumers. In the early 1990s, the advertising rate for a prime-time slot on CCTV—China's state-owned national television network—was only $60. The Wei brothers seized the opportunity offered by the low-cost advertising to bombard consumers with the Master Kong cartoon figure; in the city of Beijing, television ads appeared over a hundred times per day at their peak. At this time, many Chinese consumers avidly followed television programs from Taiwan, known for their well-crafted plots and professional production and acting. The Wei brothers positioned their advertisements in time slots immediately preceding Taiwan TV series to build an association with high-quality products from Taiwan.

After launching their advertising blitz on national television, the Weis invited the high-ranking managers of the government-owned distribution agents to attend an official product launch. That day, Ting Hsin booked three months' worth of production on its single manufacturing line. The immediate success was critical, because the brothers had convinced Ting Hsin's noodle production and packaging equipment suppliers to forgo their typical down payment in exchange for payment upon orders received. The Wei brothers initially focused their limited production on serving the Beijing market, which they quickly dominated, before expanding nationwide. They prepared for the launch of regional products with extensive product research and heavy investment in local production facilities. Within eighteen months, Ting Hsin invested over $300 million in production capacity, funded through bank debt and vendor financing.

By the end of 1994, Ting Hsin was producing over 3.3 million packets of noodles per day. In 2004, China was the largest instant noodle market in the world, accounting for nearly half of all instant noodles consumed globally (in volume). Master Kong products accounted for 33 percent of all instant noodles sold in China in volume terms, and 44 percent when measured by sales.[4] Master Kong's share of the noodle market was more than twice the second-largest competitor, Uni-President. Ting Hsin's lead over Uni-President is noteworthy. Uni-President is Taiwan's largest and historically most successful food conglomerate, founded and led by the highly regarded Taiwanese entrepreneur Chinyen Kao. Uni-President was the largest noodle producer in Taiwan, and the group's executives also saw the opportunity to sell instant noodles in China. Indeed, the company introduced its product to the market only two weeks after Master Kong's launch. In 2003, the Weis took the battle back to Taiwan when they introduced Master Kong noodles on Uni-President's home turf, seizing a 17 percent share of the market in their first year despite heavy resistance from the market leader.

Ting Hsin did many things right in entering the packaged noodle market. Unfortunately, Ting Hsin has stumbled a few times since coming to dominate the noodle market. The Wei brothers entered into several unrelated businesses, including hypermarkets, personal computer retailing, and fast-food restaurants. This diversification, among other factors, led the group to stretch its resources too thin and forced the family to seek outside financing from partners. We are not arguing that the Ting Hsin Group is a model of all aspects of managing in an unpredictable market. Ting Hsin's entry into noodles does, however, illustrate one important point that we shall discuss more generally in the remainder of the chapter.

Conduct Reconnaissance into the Future

In military parlance, reconnaissance—recon for short—describes a forward unit of an army advancing ahead of the rest of the troops to map out unfamiliar terrain, determine local circumstances (such as civilian support for the troops or the condition of roads), and locate enemy deployments that lie ahead. In describing recon, military theorists emphasize the importance of discovering the facts on the ground in real time rather than trying to impose a preexisting plan on an emerging situation. The U.S. Marines, to give a concrete example, are often thrust into rapidly changing and unfamiliar situations replete with unexpected threats and opportunities.[5] Marines spend much of their time conducting reconnaissance by groping their way through unfamiliar terrain and assessing circumstances that shift constantly with changes in weather, enemy movements, and the deployment of their own forces. Facing these conditions, Marines follow a simple rule that can be summed up as "recon pull, not headquarters push," which encourages Marines to rely on their understanding of the emerging situation based on local knowledge in real time rather than to blindly execute a preconceived plan from headquarters. This rule allows the Marines to capitalize on their local knowledge to spot opportunities and threats quickly and grants them the autonomy to improvise in response to facts on the ground.

When advancing into the fog of the future, managers should likewise conduct reconnaissance. We use the phrase *reconnaissance into the future* to describe the process of surveying a complex and rapidly changing environment to form an intuitive mental map of the emerging situation in all its complexity. Reconnaissance in the business domain requires gathering data on the myriad variables that affect a firm's performance (e.g., technology, competitive dynamics, customer preferences, government policy), anticipating emerging threats and opportunities to a firm's ability to create and sustain value, and using this information to create a mental map of the situation. This holistic map that encompasses the big picture allows managers to quickly sort the stream of data rushing in, separate the critical signals from the noise, and spot new data inconsistent with their understanding. Entrepreneurs or managers competing in a rapidly changing market should act based on this map of the emerging situation. Like troops in unfamiliar and rapidly changing terrain, their advance should be pulled by local reconnaissance into the future, rather than pushed by the headquarters' plan. The importance of discovering an emerging situation rather than imposing a preexisting plan extends not only to business and war, but also to other domains of action occurring under uncertain conditions (see the box entitled "Discover, Don't Impose").

The Wei brothers based their entry into the packaged noodle market on a deep understanding of the local food market that stemmed from two failed experiments and in-depth customer research on local tastes. Uni-President forfeited leadership in the Chinese noodle market to Ting Hsin in large part because top executives in Taiwan relied on headquarters push rather than recon pull. In contrast to the Wei brothers, Uni-President executives conducted no local taste tests before introducing their instant noodles on the mainland. Instead, the company simply introduced its best-selling shrimp-flavored noodles from Taiwan at a high price point. Chinese consumers, however, did not fancy Uni-President's shrimp-flavored noodles, nor did they see value at the prices charged. By the time Uni-President delved into the local market and rethought its product, pricing, and distribution policies, the Master Kong brand had already seized market leadership.

Discover, Don't Impose

A S PART OF my ongoing research into effective management in unpredictable markets, I have studied a variety of nonbusiness domains in which participants must advance quickly into an unpredictable future, including improvisational comedy, jazz music, warfare, sports, and scientific experimentation. These domains all require people to act in the face of an unpredictable future. An actor who has read a script knows exactly how the play will end and only needs to remember and recite his or her lines. An improvisational comedian, in contrast, must jump into the fray without knowing how the situation will unfold in real time.

Given the common need to act without knowing how things will turn out, it is not surprising that some common principles emerge across these domains. One of the most robust shared principles is one I term *discover, don't impose*. The realms of comedy, jazz, war, sports, and science each express this principle in their own language, but the underlying spirit is strikingly similar. Comedians, musicians, athletes, and warriors must resist the temptation to impose a preconceived vision on an emerging situation. Rather, they should discover the unfolding logic of a situation, anticipate what is likely to come next, and act accordingly. Hockey players, to cite a well-known adage, should skate to where the puck will be rather than where it is now.

Improvisational comedy emphasizes the same lesson in different terms. A surprising rule of thumb in improvisational comedy forbids telling jokes, which smother the emerging flow of humor by imposing a preconceived structure onto a fluid situation. Instead, experienced improvisational comics try to discover the "game"—or underlying logic—of a skit as it emerges in the early lines of dialogue. A game might consist of two actors trying to outdo one another, or saying precisely the opposite of what they think. Once a game begins to emerge, however, its logic guides subsequent action.

The importance of discovering rather than imposing is a core tenet of most of the Chinese entrepreneurs we studied and builds on deep roots in Chinese culture. From ancient times to modern, Chinese military thinking has emphasized the wisdom of discovering rather than imposing. One of the most influential chapters of Sun Tzu's *Art of War,* for example, extols the benefits of variation in tactics and of adaptability to shifting situations. Sun Tzu argued that there are roads that must not be followed, armies that must not be attacked, towns that must not be besieged, positions that must not be contested, and commands of the sovereign that must not be obeyed. The core argument is that soldiers on the front lines must improvise and adapt to the real situation in real time instead of simply implementing a preconceived strategy.

Chairman Mao demonstrated the benefit of discovering rather than imposing in the 1930s, when he ignored the doctrinaire commands of Communist International that specified Communists should lead revolutions by fostering uprising among the urban proletariat. Disregarding theoretical niceties, Mao recognized that the key to China in reality lay with peasants in the countryside. As a result of his assessment of the facts on the ground, Mao adopted the rural guerrilla warfare that ultimately provided the Chinese Communist Party with victory. All students in the People's Republic of China studied (and to this day still read) Mao's stories, and the mainland entrepreneurs we studied internalized Mao's respect for dealing with emerging circumstances in real time and disdain for plans preconceived from afar.

Of course, these domains also differ from one another and from business. Sports and war, for example, emphasize zero-sum games in which only one side can win. Improvisational comedy and jazz, in contrast, emphasize cooperation among the players. Business, of course, combines cooperation and competition. The robustness of discovering rather than imposing across these divergent domains, however, suggests its importance as a principle of effective management in unpredictable situations.

Reconnaissance into the future is critical to success in an unpredictable market such as China. But how, as a practical matter, do entrepreneurs and managers conduct reconnaissance? The following sections set forth some practical steps that managers can take to conduct reconnaissance in unpredictable contexts.

Immerse Yourself in the Situation

Uni-President executives relied on headquarters push, in part because they lacked managers immersed in the local context who could conduct recon into the future. The company's key decision makers were reluctant to leave their comfortable homes in Taiwan to live on the mainland. From the earliest days, however, three of the four Wei brothers lived on the mainland. They also built a compound in Tianjin, with 280 villas and amenities, to help executives and managers from Taiwan relocate to the mainland with their families. Avoiding headquarters push requires recon, which in turn requires immersion. Many multinationals flounder in China because key decision makers fail to immerse themselves in the local situation. Rather than granting local managers wide authority, senior executives attempt to run the Chinese subsidiary from headquarters. Even when multinationals grant the Chinese subsidiary autonomy, they often rely on expatriate managers who lack the language skills, local knowledge, or historical context to see the big picture, form a mental model of the emerging situation, and anticipate how it might unfold.

There are, of course, risks as well as benefits associated with immersion. Managers and entrepreneurs may go native, fall prey to herd mentality, or take a parochial view and ignore trends in the global market. Obviously, managers in multinationals must balance the need for immersion and recon with the imperative to efficiently use centralized resources such as a global brand or technology. In unpredictable markets, however, the advantages of immersion are so compelling that executives should generally tip the balance toward recon pull. Three advantages of immersion are particularly important:

- *Spotting opportunities and threats.* Discerning opportunities and threats before they are obvious to everyone else requires firsthand knowledge of local circumstances. This direct knowledge of local circumstances is particularly important in rapidly changing situations where knowledge can grow stale very quickly.

- *Building a holistic picture.* In unpredictable markets, managers must discern the critical few variables from a tidal wave of less relevant factors. In ambiguous markets like China, however, the distinction between central and peripheral factors is not clear-cut and may change regularly. In China, government agencies may change the rules in the middle of the game, new competitors may emerge from unexpected places, and, of course, technology may shift. To distinguish between central and peripheral variables that shift over time, managers and entrepreneurs must expose themselves to the full range of factors influencing their company, which is impossible from a detached perspective.

- *Having a stake in the outcome.* Managers who are on the ground generally have a stake in the outcome of the local business. A stake in the outcome of the local company not only provides incentives to work harder but also heightens the emotional engagement required to notice, weigh, and process all the data in a complex, rapidly changing situation. A detached observer with nothing to gain or lose will lack the edge in sensing which variables matter most, because the cost of getting it wrong is lower.

Keep the Map Fluid

Reconnaissance into the future must be a mindful activity. The mental model must remain fluid and evolve continuously as the situation itself changes, and managers must avoid the temptation to fixate on data that confirm their expectations while ignoring information that doesn't fit. The key to successful recon lies in alertness to surprises, anomalies, and unexpected findings. These often provide the early warnings of forthcoming golden opportunities or sudden-death threats. Like troops conducting recon for possible threats from and opportunities to attack the enemy, managers must remain alert to what seems out of place. People tend to focus on the snapshot of a situation at a point in time—the *content* of a company's strategy. The critical factor over time—particularly in dynamic markets such as China—is the *process* of forming and updating the picture as circumstances change.[6]

Make no mistake—conducting recon into the future is a mentally taxing task. Managers must rapidly identify early warning signals, see fresh connections among apparently unrelated events, and find the needles of key variables in the haystacks of less critical ones. They must conduct these tasks based on incomplete and often conflicting information in real time. Military theorists often compare this task to the knack for seeing a few pieces of a jigsaw puzzle and rapidly grasping what the overall picture must look like. This comparison simplifies the capability, however, because it implies that there is a single "right" interpretation of a situation. In unpredictable environments, however, there is no single right answer at any point in time. Moreover, even the best map may outlive its utility as the situation evolves. A better metaphor would be the skill of observing a seemingly random assortment of Lego blocks and seeing a possible construction that is superior to competitors'. Here are a few tips on keeping a map fluid:

- *Put a dashboard on the race car.* If competing in China resembles a race car driving in the fog, then a dashboard of financial and operating metrics is critical to staying in the flow of information. These data must be *real time*, of course, but should also provide *multiple perspectives* on the company to help managers spot early tremors and make connections. The data should also be *fine-grained*, because highly aggregated data can hide threats and opportunities by melding results from multiple operating units, product lines, or geographies. Managers can avoid drowning in a sea of information by focusing on a relatively small number of critical variables for intense scrutiny. The choice of critical factors depends on the current mental model of the situation and will shift over time as the map itself evolves. Noncritical metrics can be monitored on a variance basis (i.e., by focusing on differences between actual performance and expectations) to spot anomalies and surprises early on.

- *Interrogate anomalies.* Most people walk through life shrugging off unexpected events. Wei was not the first person to eat tasty noodles on a train or to attract other passengers' attention in a packed passenger car. He was, however, apparently the first to see this as a potential market opportunity to introduce packaged noodles in China. Surprises are important. Having a mental map allows managers to notice *anomalies*—unexpected events that are not as they should be according to the manager's assessment of the situation.[7] Small anomalies often serve as leading indicators of either impending threats or opportunities, and managers who see them earlier than others can anticipate looming changes and respond more quickly and effectively. Like a sailor running aground on an island that doesn't show up on the map, these events tell us that our map is wrong, and updating it faster than rivals may confer a competitive advantage for a time. Rather than shrugging anomalies off, managers should ask a few critical questions each time they are surprised: Is this a potential opportunity? Is this a potential threat? What can I do to find out more?

- *Take field trips to the future.* Chinese entrepreneurs often glean insights into the likely development trajectory of their industry by studying how the industry has evolved in more developed countries. The Wei brothers, of course, were steeped in Taiwan's sophisticated food industry before moving to the mainland, while Sina's Wang visited Silicon Valley to see where the information technology industry in China might move. Managers can learn much from these field trips to the future, including the ultimate level of concentration, eventual consumer penetration, and the critical resources required to succeed in the future (e.g., brand, technology, economies of scale, economies of scope). There also is much that managers cannot learn from these field trips to the future, including the timing, pace, and exact path of evolution. "History doesn't repeat itself," as Mark Twain observed, "but it rhymes." Because the evolution of industries will not repeat itself identically, managers must apply judgment and prudence in applying what they learn on their field trips.

- *Move beyond the obvious.* Improvisational comedians follow a rule of thumb to "avoid the obvious joke." If a joke is obvious to the comedian, it will be obvious—and boring—to the audience as well. A similar logic applies in conducting recon, where obvious is also a four-letter word. If something seems obvious to managers, it is likely to be obvious to competitors, who will almost certainly be responding accordingly. By the time a threat or opportunity is obvious, it may already be too late. Managers can take active steps to avoid the obvious. Top executives at China's pioneering Internet systems integrator and software developer AsiaInfo, for example, pass on any opportunities where the customer can articulate both the problem and the solution. By the time both problem and solution are obvious, rivals will already be pursuing the opportunity. Rather, the AsiaInfo managers focus on opportunities where the customer can articulate the pain but not yet spell out the solution.

Trust Your Gut (But Digest Plenty of Data)

Forming a mental model of a rapidly changing situation is primarily an intuitive—not analytical—process.[8] Analysis, by definition, dissects things into their component parts for closer inspection. Reconnaissance, in contrast, demands managers maintain a sense of the big picture to spot anomalies. Clarity about the nature of the situation generally comes as a sudden burst of insight rather than from a systematic analysis. Methodical data collection and analysis, of course, play a role in informing these intuitive leaps, but so do countless other less formal sources of data, both planned and accidental. Often the most important insights into a situation stem from making fresh connections among variables that appear unrelated at first glance. Sina's success in short message services, for instance, resulted from top executives seeing mobile phones as a way to collect payment on small transactions in a country where few people have credit cards. Intuition also helps managers and entrepreneurs discern the few critical variables from among the countless less important details.

To conduct reconnaissance in a complex, dynamic, interactive environment, managers must sense their surroundings. *Sense* is an odd word to choose—one might have expected a term that stresses systematic search, such as *study* or *investigate*. Sense, however, emphasizes the intuitive aspect of data gathering and processing. In some cases, of course, managers will know precisely the data they need. Once the Wei brothers decided to enter the instant noodle market, for example, they conducted systematic research on consumer preferences. In an unpredictable market, however, entrepreneurs or managers often do not know what they do not know. In these cases, they must sense their surroundings, be alert to anomalies, and be open to new interpretations. Ting Hsin would never have entered noodles in the first place if it hadn't been for Yin-Heng's "aha" moment on the train. The most important implication for managers is that they must trust their gut instinct in making decisions in unpredictable markets.

Let us be very clear: this is not an argument against analysis. Many Chinese entrepreneurs rely solely on their gut instinct. Frankly, these are not the ones that Western managers must worry about, since they generally start quick, rise fast, and crash early. The most formidable Chinese entrepreneurs are those—like the Weis—who use intuition *informed by* analysis, not *instead of* analysis. They trust their gut because they digest plenty of data. Ing-Chou—the oldest Wei brother—takes this quite literally, sampling a few packages of instant noodles from various Ting Hsin factories every morning to ensure high quality. Ting Hsin managers are even known to rummage through trash barrels to inspect what brands people are eating (and finishing).

Incorporate Multiple Perspectives

Many Chinese entrepreneurs adopt the "Great Leader" approach in managing their businesses. The company is basically an extension of the founder, who gathers his own data, forms a map of the situation, and makes all the important decisions based on his own mental model. This Great Leader approach has a long precedent in Chinese society, from the ancient emperors down to Chairmen Mao and Deng, and provides significant advantages. The founder can make decisions quickly and execute them efficiently. If the Great Leader's ability to conduct recon into the future is consistently better than competitors', the company (or country) will prosper. This is the model followed by a few of the successful entrepreneurs we studied, such as Qinghou Zong of Wahaha, and is quite common among Chinese entrepreneurs more broadly.

The Great Leader approach has risks. This model does not scale easily, because the founder's time and attention are stretched too thin if he or she tries to remain involved in every decision as the company grows. There is also the challenge of succession—what happens to the company when the Great Leader is no longer around? Perhaps the greatest limitation of this approach is that the company's success relies on one individual's perspective on the situation. The founder will, of course, solicit and listen to other people's views, but at the end of the day he or she will make all the big decisions. This leaves the company vulnerable to the idiosyncrasies, blind spots, and biases of a single individual.

One of the great innovations of Western entrepreneurship has been an alternative model of top management in which decisions incorporate multiple perspectives. This team model is particularly common among start-ups backed by venture capital firms, which fund new companies but in return secure the board seats and ownership to influence the composition of the company's top management team. Recall how Sina's venture capitalists urged Wang to bring in professional managers and ultimately replaced him when the challenges facing the company no longer matched his strengths.

The primary advantage of the team approach is that it incorporates multiple perspectives into the process of sensing the environment and digesting new information. A strong chief financial officer, for example, might anticipate when a window of opportunity for raising capital might open and allow the company to steal a march on its rivals. Savvy venture capitalists can spot common emerging threats that they've encountered in other portfolio companies, or can make connections across companies, as Daniel Mao did in connecting the leading mainland and American Chinese Web sites. Viewing the world from their different perspectives allows the team to collectively form a richer mental model of a complex situation. This was the approach taken by Tingyi. Initially the four Wei brothers specialized, with the oldest focusing on operations, the second on business relations, the third on finance, and the youngest on marketing. Later, the Weis assembled a team of strong functional managers from companies that included Nestlé and Taiwan Semiconductor Manufacturing Company (TSMC).

Design and Conduct Conscious Experiments

Sometimes managers don't know what they don't know, and as a result must rely on surprise to find out if their assessment of the situation is off. Often, however, they *do* know what they don't know and can actively design experiments to fill in the gaps in their knowledge.[9] We define an experiment as a low-cost test designed to reduce key sources of uncertainty prior to committing additional resources. Entrepreneurs and managers run low-cost experiments all the time, including such actions as prototyping products or launching a service in one city or province before rolling it out nationally. Entrepreneurs and managers often learn less than they could from these tests, however, because they do not identify the key sources of uncertainty before running the experiment. Some ways to design experiments more effectively follow.

- *Identify deal killers and big bets.* Entrepreneurs and managers can often identify *deal killer* risks that would render a new opportunity unviable. The Wei brothers identified price as a deal killer for instant noodles after learning that all the advertising and quality in the world couldn't make their oil or egg rolls work if they were too expensive. Entrepreneurs and managers can also identify the key variables that would drive the upside in the opportunity. A simple way to spot these is to ask "what are we betting on here?" These *big bets* could be superior technology, a critical relationship, or the ability to move faster than rivals, to name just a few examples. In the Ting Hsin case, superior taste is the big bet driving the upside. Tingyi conducts a blind taste test relative to competitors' offerings and will only launch a product if 70 percent of the tasters prefer Master Kong. These experiments afford the company a 20 percent success rate on new product launches, compared with the industry average of 5 percent. It is easier to design and execute effective experiments if managers and entrepreneurs are clear about deal killers and big bets.

- *Cap your investment and time.* Sometimes experiments can take on a life of their own. Managers can avoid experiment creep by setting a limit on time and expenses, with the intent to test and review findings before spending more. When computer maker Legend faced the onslaught of multinationals in the 1990s, for example, the company gave itself one year to run an experiment to see if it could survive in the new competitive environment. If it could not succeed in one year, it committed to closing its PC business in China.

- *Stage your experiments.* Whenever possible, it is better to run cheaper experiments before running more expensive experiments. This allows managers and entrepreneurs to benefit from the new knowledge prior to investing additional resources. Ting Hsin's entry into noodles exemplifies staging experiments: the Wei brothers first conducted a small taste test, and then converted an existing line and launched Master Kong noodles in Beijing. It was only after this cheap experiment proved wildly successful that the Wei brothers invested in further advertising, production facilities, and distribution for a national rollout to test whether the noodles would sell outside Beijing.

- *Conduct multiple experiments.* In a turbulent environment, managers don't know beforehand which opportunities will turn out to be golden and which will be threats that could prove their undoing. Some options that look promising initially will fizzle out, and threats that appear inconsequential may emerge as critical. Given this unpredictability, managers must run multiple experiments rather than focusing on a single potential opportunity or threat. A prudent general does not send out scouts in a single direction, but rather conducts recon along several paths that the army might end up following. Running too many experiments simultaneously, however, can distract managers' attention and prevent them from processing the information produced by their actions. If these experiments are costly, moreover, they stretch the company's resources too thin. Ting Hsin diversified widely in the mid-1990s into hypermarkets, fast-food restaurants, rice cakes, and various beverages, thereby spreading the group's limited resources too thin. In general, a company should run no more than a couple of major experiments simultaneously.

- *Allocate good people to experiments.* Top executives are often tempted to send "expendable" employees as scouts to run experiments, rather than removing valuable managers from their positions. Inexperienced managers, however, are prone to exhaust themselves too quickly or, more important, to fail to recognize a promising opportunity when it arises. Ting Hsin sent one of the four Wei brothers to explore China, whereas Uni-President kept its best managers in Taiwan initially.

Summary

Managers can improve their odds of succeeding in an unpredictable market by conducting reconnaissance into the future rather than relying on a preconceived plan from headquarters. Managers can take several concrete steps to conduct recon into the future, which are summarized in the following list. Conducting recon into the future does not alone guarantee success. Rather, executives must translate their mental map of the emerging situation into concrete priorities to execute effectively. The next chapter introduces the sense-anticipate-prioritize-execute cycle to do just that.

- *Reconnaissance into the future* describes the process of gathering data on the myriad variables that affect a firm's performance in order create an intuitive mental map of the situation in its full complexity and spot anomalies that could signal emerging threats or opportunities.

- *Recon pull versus headquarters push* is a rule of thumb that implies entrepreneurs or managers competing in a rapidly changing market should rely on their understanding of the emerging situation based on local knowledge in real time rather than blindly executing a preconceived plan from headquarters.

- *Immerse yourself in the situation.* Multinationals often flounder in emerging markets such as China because key decision makers fail to immerse themselves in the local situation, instead attempting to run a local subsidiary from headquarters. Even when multinationals grant the local subsidiary autonomy, they often rely on expatriate managers who lack the language skills, local knowledge, or historical context to form a mental model of the emerging situation and anticipate how it might unfold.

- *Keep the map fluid,* because the key to successful recon lies in alertness to surprises, anomalies, and unexpected findings.

These often provide the early warnings of forthcoming golden opportunities or sudden-death threats and form the basis for revising the map.

- *Trust your gut (but digest plenty of data).* Forming a mental model of a rapidly changing situation is primarily an intuitive—not analytical—process, and managers must trust their gut instinct in making decisions in unpredictable markets. Intuition, however, must be informed by data and analysis.

- *Incorporate multiple perspectives* into the process of gathering new information and digesting what it means for the company. Multiple perspectives allow the top management team to form a richer model of a complex situation, while functional experts can better and more quickly sense emerging threats or opportunities in their specific domain.

- *Design and conduct conscious experiments* to test "deal killer" sources of uncertainty.

FOUR

Outcycle the Competition

THE LAST CHAPTER argued that conducting reconnaissance into the future is necessary for surviving and thriving in an unpredictable market. But forming a mental map of a fluid situation and anticipating looming threats and opportunities is not enough. Entrepreneurs and managers must translate their insight into effective and timely action. The ash heap of business history overflows with the remains of companies whose leaders spotted threats or opportunities but failed to respond with sufficient speed or vigor.

This chapter discusses how successful companies move from insight to action in unpredictable markets. It introduces the *SAPE cycle*, named after its constituent steps: managers *sense* the overall situation, *anticipate* emerging threats and opportunities, *prioritize* necessary actions, and *execute* these priorities in a timely and effective manner. We argue that competition in unpredictable markets is best conceptualized as repeated rounds in which companies move through successive iterations of the SAPE cycle and compete to seize new opportunities and respond to emergent threats. Over time, a company that successfully outcycles its competition gains a cumulative advantage that can prove decisive, although each of the individual moves may provide only an incremental lead. Viewing competition as rounds of time-competitive SAPE cycles explains success in unpredictable environments more convincingly than common explanations such as long-term vision, a grand strategy, or some decisive strategic move.

We illustrate our argument by comparing the histories of Legend and Great Wall between their foundation in the mid-1980s and 1999, when Legend emerged as the undisputed leader in China's personal computer market while Great Wall faded into relative obscurity. Legend Group Ltd. is one of the great success stories of China's first generation of entrepreneurs.[1] The Beijing-based Legend (which changed its English brand name to Lenovo in 2003 and its English company name to the Lenovo Group in 2004) is the largest information technology company in the People's Republic of China, booking revenues of approximately $3 billion in fiscal year 2004. Its branded personal computer has been the country's best-selling PC since 1997, with a market share of over 27 percent at year-end 2003.[2] At that time, Lenovo was also the number one PC brand in Asia Pacific (including Japan), with a regional market share of 12.6 percent, and the company's strong position in Asia earned it a place among the top ten computer companies in the world. In recent years, Legend has entered into several new market segments, including online services, information technology consulting, and mobile phone handsets, which have started to contribute modestly to the company's bottom line. Legend's dramatic rise took place in the span of a few years, with its share of the domestic PC market rising from 6.9 percent in 1996 to 27 percent by 2003. During this time period, Legend pulled ahead of global PC leaders such as IBM, Hewlett-Packard, AST, Acer, and Compaq in the Chinese market. Legend also left domestic leader Great Wall in the dust.

Legend and Great Wall Computer began their corporate lives as very similar companies. Both were founded in Beijing in the early 1980s and had strong affiliations with government agencies that provided access to homegrown information technology and a mandate to develop the computer industry in China. Legend was founded by

Mr. Chuanzhi Liu and funded by China's Academy of Science, whereas Great Wall was closely affiliated with the Ministry of Electronic Industries (MEI). Both new enterprises started with limited financial and human resources.

Despite their similar beginnings, Great Wall pulled out to an early lead in the 1980s and appeared well positioned to maintain its head start in China's personal computer market. Great Wall developed and commercialized the first add-on card to read Chinese characters and enjoyed an initial monopoly. Great Wall's close connections with the MEI allowed the company to obtain one of the first licenses to manufacture personal computers in China. Legend, in contrast, was initially unable to secure the production authorization needed to manufacture PCs in China's planned economy. Legend's founders instead set up a subsidiary in Hong Kong to first make motherboards and later assemble PCs. By the late 1980s, Great Wall had established itself as the top PC brand in China, well ahead of Legend. Great Wall was also a technology leader, introducing the first domestic PC with Intel-based 286 and 386 processors inside. By 1999, however, Legend was China's number one PC brand with 20.1 percent of the domestic market, while Great Wall's share had slid to under 5 percent.

What accounted for this dramatic reversal in fortune? This is not an Apple versus PC story. Legend and Great Wall both ran the Windows operating system on Intel chips. In explaining Legend's rise relative to Great Wall, commentators have tended to focus on the decisive years between 1996 and 1999, when Legend's market share skyrocketed while Great Wall's drifted downward. And indeed, Legend's actions during this period were critical. The foundations for Legend's success, however, were laid much earlier as the company repeatedly outcycled Great Wall as they jointly faced a series of threats and opportunities in the fast-moving PC market in China.

The Rise of a Legend

When Chuanzhi Liu graduated from the Xi'an Military Communications Engineering College in 1966, he looked forward to a career as an engineer. Liu had the misfortune, however, to graduate during

China's Cultural Revolution. Born into an intellectual family, Liu was not considered a member of the working class and was therefore designated for reeducation. After a one-year stint at the Commission of Science, Technology, and Industry for National Defense in Chengdu city, Liu was forced to work as a laborer on a state-owned rice farm from 1968 to 1970.

After two years of farmwork in the southern province of Guangdong, Liu was permitted to take a position as an engineer with the Institute of Computing Technology (ICT) of the Chinese Academy of Sciences (CAS), where he spent the next thirteen years conducting research on magnetic recording circuits. Although Liu won several awards for his innovations, he grew increasingly frustrated by the lack of practical application for the technology he developed and by the large gap between the prototypes he developed and existing Western products. Liu later recalled his frustration: "To a great extent, our research was used only to demonstrate China's level of research ability compared to the U.S and the Soviet Union. However, the research had no practical purpose, and was not turned into products. We technicians wrote papers to demonstrate the performance of the machine, so that we could be promoted, and earn extra salary . . . But once a project was closed, no attention was placed on the research result, and we immediately started a new program. We did not convert our achievements into products or make the technology widely available."

Liu's opportunity came with a change in government regulation that permitted the creation of quasi-private enterprises in the early 1980s. In the wake of this new policy, university researchers left their jobs to start new ventures in Zhongguancun, where some of them earned more in a day than they could in a month at a state-run university or research institute. In 1984, ICT's director established a new venture to commercialize the institute's technology and use the money earned thereby to fund the institute's research and supplement engineers' salaries to stem the brain drain. Impressed by Liu's managerial skills, the director chose him to lead the newly formed New Technology Development Company of the Chinese Academy of Sciences, or NTD for short. Liu—then 40 years old—started off with ten other researchers, about $57,000 in start-up capital, and a small office contributed by the ICT.

The Early Years

Although the Institute of Computing Technology of CAS had developed many sophisticated technologies, few of them found immediate commercial applications in the first few years. To pay the bills, Liu established NTD as a small-scale distributor, purchasing computer products from government importers and reselling them to state-owned enterprises. Margins in this business, however, were depressed by gray-market resellers who avoided taxes and tariffs by smuggling computers into China and then gained market share by charging lower prices. Liu anticipated that remaining an undifferentiated distributor would not be a sustainable business and began to look for ways to differentiate NTD.

Technology was the obvious solution. In 1987, the company introduced an add-on card under the Legend brand that allowed Chinese applications to run on English-language operating systems. As you will recall from the Sina case, many Chinese companies at this time were developing software solutions to bridge the gap with English-language operating systems, but the Legend Chinese-character card was distinctive in two ways. First, the product—which could be inserted directly into a PC's motherboard—combined hardware and software, an approach that conserved scarce memory and prevented the piracy common to software-only solutions. Second, the Legend Chinese-character card incorporated proprietary character-recognition software (developed by ICT scientists) that prompted users with likely Chinese characters based on their earlier entries, thereby saving significant time in data entry.

The Legend Chinese-character card was a great success, and within two years accounted for approximately one-third of company revenues; the established distribution business contributed most of the remainder. In 1989, Liu renamed NTD Legend after its best-known product, and the Legend Group was born. The success of the Chinese-character card provided NTD with the credibility to sign deals to distribute Hewlett-Packard (HP) printers and AST personal computers bundled with its card. The distribution deals were non-exclusive, so Legend had to develop marketing and sales capabilities to differentiate itself from other distributors used by multinationals. Liu and his colleagues quickly mastered marketing and sales and helped the U.S.-based AST to pull ahead of larger rivals such as IBM, Compaq, and Acer in China. By the early 1990s, AST had carved out approximately 30 percent of the Chinese market, which was nearly twice the percentage share of number two Compaq.

Legend's success in distributing AST's products along with its expertise in marketing and sales stoked Liu's aspiration to build a Legend-brand PC. Although Liu was confident Legend could produce PCs, he failed to convince government officials. In the late 1980s, the Ministry of Electronic Industries was responsible for China's domestic personal computer market and held the power to grant or deny manufacturing licenses for computers. Legend—then a small player and unaffiliated with the MEI—could not secure a production license. Great Wall, in contrast, enjoyed a cozy relationship with MEI and obtained a license to manufacture its own-brand personal computers. In exchange for the license and MEI support, Great Wall was required to source components (excluding chips) locally. By the early 1990s, Great Wall was the largest domestic producer of PCs and had built three new production facilities in expectation of growing demand.

Rebuffed on the mainland, Liu set his sights on Hong Kong. In 1988, he established Legend Hong Kong as a joint venture with Dow Computer Systems Limited and China Technology Trade (H. K. Limited). Legend Hong Kong acquired a motherboard manufacturing company and aggressively ramped up development and production of motherboards and add-on cards to gain expertise in global sourcing of components and in assembling the guts of a personal computer. The next year, a delegation of senior Chinese trade officials visited Legend's booth at a trade fair in Germany and were favorably impressed by what they saw. After conducting due diligence of the Hong Kong operations, the MEI authorized Legend to commence PC production on the mainland in 1990. Six years after leaving the Institute of Computing Technology, Liu had achieved his dream of producing a branded PC in China.

Surviving the Sudden-Death Threat of Multinational Entry

Legend entered China's PC market at a difficult time. When the company began producing computers on the mainland in 1990, imported computers accounted for slightly less than one-third of PC unit shipments. Within two years, however, imports' share jumped to nearly two-thirds of the total market. Several factors contributed to the multinationals' surge. In 1992, the Chinese government signed a far-reaching trade agreement with the United States that sharply lowered import tariffs on a range of electronic and information technology products and peripherals. This change in policy coincided with slowing demand in the developed markets, which spurred Western companies such as Compaq, IBM, Acer, and HP to look abroad for growth. Many industry analysts believed that the Chinese market—with PC sales of only 100,000 units in 1991—was poised for explosive growth. Multinationals could leverage their technology, brand, and global economies of scale to offer high-quality, low-cost products that domestic producers found hard to match.

Just as Legend was establishing itself on the mainland, it faced an onslaught from multinationals that threatened its very survival, and indeed the existence of China's domestic PC industry overall. The year 1993 was a low point in Legend's history. In the face of heightened competition from multinationals and domestic companies desperate to protect their position, Legend missed its sales goal for the first time ever. As if that weren't enough, an equipment supplier absconded with a large sum of money, and Liu himself spent months tracking him down to retrieve the cash. Key managers were considering leaving the company. The company's difficulties exacted a physical toll on Liu, who was hospitalized for three months.

When Liu's health permitted, he would convene his management team and rally the troops in his hospital room. He spent a great deal of time attempting to convince Yuanqing Yang, a promising young manager, to abandon his plans to go abroad and instead to remain with Legend. Liu argued that Yang's departure would not only jeopardize Legend's future but also the future of China's national computer industry, which could be wiped out by multinationals. Yang agreed to stay, and Liu appointed the twenty-nine-year-old as general manager of Legend's PC business.

Legend's top management team agreed to see if the PC business could survive as an independent entity in the new environment and pledged to close the business or enter into a partnership if they could not make it work after one year. The business press was openly skeptical of Liu's decision and questioned whether Legend's leaders had allowed patriotism to cloud their business judgment. Yang, however, was undaunted and lost no time after taking the helm in early 1994. He quickly surrounded himself with a team of young managers and consolidated the formerly independent functional units into a single PC business unit, linking managers' bonuses to business unit performance to align incentives and improve coordination across the units.

Yang and his team launched a series of basic operating and financial improvements in rapid-fire succession: They strengthened relations with dealers by increasing transparency and eliminating competitive direct sales. They improved product quality. Legend freed working capital by cutting accounts receivable to thirty days (versus an industry average of ninety days) and increasing inventory turns from 1.7 to 7 times per year.[3] To bolster its financial reserves, the company raised approximately $27 million in an initial public offering of its equity on the Hong Kong stock exchange. Legend survived its one-year experiment during 1994. Indeed, the company continued to hang on during the subsequent years, and even eked out a slight increase in market share, from 6.3 percent in 1992 to 6.9 percent in 1996.

Great Wall, in contrast, saw its market share slip from nearly 11 percent to just over 2 percent over the same time period. Great Wall managers did not, of course, freeze like deer in the headlights of an oncoming car during this period. In fact, the company's leaders took many of the same actions as Legend. Unfortunately, they were consistently slower in initiating operating and financial improvements and less aggressive in executing them. Like Legend, Great Wall also raised much-needed equity, but made its initial public offering on the Shenzhen market three years after Legend. Great Wall, for example, was slow to improve product quality because it relied on domestic components suppliers, who often exported their best parts for hard currency and shipped what was left to Great Wall. Legend, in contrast, had always relied on global suppliers for key components. Part of Great Wall's slowness in making needed operational and financial improvements may have resulted from its joint venture with IBM. The company entered into protracted negotiations over the ownership structure of the joint venture (which was ultimately resolved with IBM controlling 51 percent of the combined entity to Great Wall's 49 percent) and subsequently needed to coordinate major decisions with IBM's global management.

Seizing the Golden Opportunity: 1996 to 1999

By 1996, Legend had not only survived the sudden-death threat, but had positioned itself for future growth. The company had put in place processes as efficient as its global competitors. The executives who lived through the hard years were now seasoned industry veterans. By maintaining its share of a rapidly growing market, Legend had increased unit production volumes to the level at which it began to enjoy purchasing and manufacturing economies of scale. The company had even accumulated a modest war chest of cash on the balance sheet to fund future investments. Great Wall, in contrast, continued to struggle and was poorly positioned to seize new opportunities as they arose.

Foreign brands continued to dominate China's market through the mid-1990s. The Legend management team, however, conducted careful analysis of the multinationals' competitive strengths and weaknesses and came to the conclusion that they were "paper tigers" (a Maoist term describing enemies who appear invincible but are in fact weak and could be defeated). HP, IBM, Compaq, and Acer all followed the same rules of competition. They charged global rates for their products, which priced PCs beyond the budget of most

Chinese consumers. The computer companies targeted the enterprise market, which consisted of state-owned firms, government agencies, and joint ventures with multinationals that could afford the pricey machines. The Western companies believed it was not worth the effort to design PCs tailored to the Chinese market. Despite its high percentage growth on a low base, in the mid-1990s China still accounted for only about 2 to 3 percent of the global market for PC units. Multinationals also used China as a dumping ground for their outdated technology, generally introducing new models to China one or two quarters after introducing them in developed markets.

Legend's executives saw the transition from Intel 486 to Pentium chips as a golden opportunity to overtake the Western companies. In early 1996, Legend introduced a Pentium-based PC in China at the same time that Compaq, IBM, and other producers were launching Pentium PCs in the United States and Western Europe. This early launch in China allowed Legend to win high-end users. Legend coupled its new product introduction with a 30 percent price reduction on the 486 technology to win market share, particularly in the consumer market, and followed that with more price reductions. The multinationals failed to match Legend's price cuts, perhaps because executives viewed these cuts as a desperate ploy by a failing company. Legend also introduced a series of new products tailored to Chinese consumers.

In the final quarter of 1996, Legend pulled ahead of IBM in market share, an accomplishment that attracted great media attention in China and fueled the company's momentum, particularly among home users. Legend's increased volume conferred additional economies of scale in purchasing, distribution, and assembly that allowed the company to offer further price cuts. Legend continued to offer products tailored to the local market and to benefit from the publicity of being a local David beating the global Goliaths. By 1999, Legend was the clear leader in the Chinese market with over 21.5 percent market share, compared with 6 to 7 percent for HP and IBM, a leadership position that Legend has maintained to this day.

In 2004, Lenovo (recall the name change) remained the undisputed leader in China's PC market but found itself once again in a period of active waiting. The company faces potential sudden-death threats such as the aggressive growth of Dell, which has experienced great success with its direct sales model in China. Early in 2004, top management reaffirmed their commitment to the core PC business, where it sees the potential for future growth in revenues and profits. Lenovo is also constantly experimenting with potential opportunities, although not all of its early experiments have succeeded (e.g., online services, information technology services). Lenovo now faces a hard truth of unpredictable markets: victory in the last round is no guarantee of future success. Regardless of what Lenovo's future holds, there is no question that its progress to date represents one of the more impressive tales of entrepreneurship in China.

The SAPE Cycle

While Legend raised its market share from 6 percent to 20.1 percent between 1992 and 1999, Great Wall saw its share slip from 11 percent to 4 percent over the same time period. What accounts for the very different endings for two companies with such similar beginnings? Legend's success did not result from a strategic master stroke by Legend or a blunder by Great Wall. Nor does the explanation lie in the companies' differing long-term vision: both aspired to leadership in China's PC market. Rather, the difference in their relative performance was the cumulative effect of a series of actions taken over more than a decade. Some of these actions—such as launching the Pentium PC—were strategic, many were operational. Some responded to threats, others to emerging opportunities. Consistently throughout its history, however, Legend executives did a better job of conducting reconnaissance into the future, anticipating likely threats and opportunities, and acting more quickly and effectively than their counterparts at Great Wall.

Sounds great, but how, as a practical matter, can entrepreneurs and managers emulate Legend's approach and consistently translate their understanding of a fluid situation into effective organizational action? The sense-anticipate-prioritize-execute (SAPE) cycle is a practical process that entrepreneurs and managers can use to succeed in an unpredictable market (figure 4-1). To begin, managers *sense* the current circumstances to form a holistic mental model of the overall situation; they then *anticipate* emerging opportunities and threats. These two steps should sound familiar, because they are components of conducting reconnaissance into the future.

Sensing the overall situation and anticipating opportunities and threats are necessary to survive and thrive in unpredictable markets. But they are far from sufficient. A company must also respond quickly and effectively to seize fleeting opportunities, deal with looming threats, and make necessary operating improvements. Managers can bridge the gap between anticipation and effective action by setting clear *priorities*. In unpredictable environments, entrepreneurs and managers must continuously reevaluate their priorities and be willing to alter them as circumstances change. In the final step, the entire organization *executes* against priorities. (The next chapter introduces the concept of a *flexible hierarchy* as an organizational form well suited to executing against priorities.)

FIGURE 4-1

The SAPE cycle

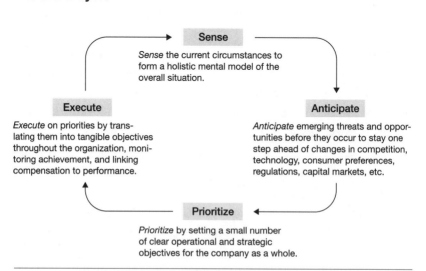

Sense

Sense the current circumstances to form a holistic mental model of the overall situation.

Execute

Execute on priorities by translating them into tangible objectives throughout the organization, monitoring achievement, and linking compensation to performance.

Anticipate

Anticipate emerging threats and opportunities before they occur to stay one step ahead of changes in competition, technology, consumer preferences, regulations, capital markets, etc.

Prioritize

Prioritize by setting a small number of clear operational and strategic objectives for the company as a whole.

Advantages of the SAPE Cycle

The SAPE model provides an alternative to the formal strategic planning process found in many—if not most—companies. An annual survey by the international consulting firm Bain & Company has found that strategic planning processes are the single most common management tool used by the companies it tracks. In 2002, 80 percent of firms surveyed utilized formal planning processes.[4] Strategic planning is widely used, but it is also largely irrelevant—at least in helping firms seize opportunities and respond to threats in unpredictable markets. Extensive research over the past twenty-five years has found no clear link between formal strategic planning and a firm's financial performance.[5]

We believe that a company's strategic planning process often falters in rapidly changing environments because it is too linear, attempts to impose a preconceived strategy on an emergent situation, divorces strategy from operations, fails to align the company with the importance of time and timing, and focuses on big bets rather than cumulative advantages. The SAPE cycle, in contrast, can help companies survive and thrive in a fast-changing environment because it is explicitly iterative. Priorities are set based on changes in the competitive situation, and they incorporate both strategic decisions and operating improvements. Finally, the process is explicitly time competitive and integrates the cumulative benefits of iterative competition.

- *Iterative versus one time.* The SAPE cycle is not meant to be a linear process like that implicit in the fortress view of time. In contrast to the fortress view, managers cannot expect to gaze deep into the future, identify an industry position that will be attractive for years to come, systematically build the resources and competencies to fortify the position, and then sustain their advantage into the indefinite future. Rather, companies must circle through each step repeatedly: managers must update their mental map of the situation based on new developments, anticipate new threats and opportunities, shift priorities in light of changing circumstances, and execute promptly and aggressively against these new objectives.

The SAPE cycle does not consider threats and opportunities as exceptions. Rather, it assumes that the situation will shift constantly and that managers must regularly update their understanding and priorities in light of new events. The trick is not getting it right once and for all. Rather, companies survive and thrive in unpredictable environments to the extent they anticipate emerging opportunities and threats and respond to them effectively *repeatedly over time*. Legend did not beat Great Wall because it started with a superior grand vision, but rather because it iterated through the SAPE cycle more effectively and quickly.

- *Situation pull versus process push.* Most established companies have some annual process for setting strategy, which drives strategic thinking for the rest of the year. The problem with these processes, however, is that important events in the industry are unlikely to coincide with stages in the annual process. Even in companies with sophisticated planning, few strategic decisions result from the process. Rather, firms respond to opportunities and threats as they arise and later incorporate these into their plan after the fact.[6]

  In unpredictable environments such as China's PC market in the 1990s, customers, competitors, regulators, and the pace of technical change determine the important contours of the emerging situation. To survive and thrive in a rapidly changing industry, a company must respond to threats and opportunities more rapidly and effectively than its rivals *as they arise*. This requires managers to be pulled into iterating through the SAPE cycle by changes in the situation, rather than to be pushed by a preordained process.

- *Strategic and operational.* Many books on strategy downplay operational improvements, whereas prominent books on execution take strategy as given. However, both are critical to success in an unpredictable environment; which is best at any

moment depends on the demands of the situation. Legend
pulled ahead of Great Wall by shifting its priorities between
operating improvements and strategic issues based on the situation. The priorities in the early 1990s were cutting working
capital and costs to survive the sudden-death threat posed by
the influx of multinationals. The late 1990s, in contrast, were
a land grab for market leadership through new product introductions and price cuts when the booming PC market in China
provided a golden opportunity. The SAPE process accommo-
dates both strategic and operational priorities. Seizing golden
opportunities or responding to sudden-death threats is critical
to success in turbulent environments, but pursuing operating
efficiency is equally critical. Operating improvements put cash
in the bank that allows a company to seize golden opportunities when they arise and to weather sudden-death threats. Less
efficient rivals emerge too enervated to compete effectively
in the next round of competition. The rapid and effective execution of operating improvements is particularly critical in
periods of active waiting to position a company for future
sudden-death threats and golden opportunities.

- *Time-competitive execution.* By and large, it is not the case
  that Legend succeeded by taking steps that Great Wall failed
  to do. In fact, Great Wall often imitated steps taken by Legend. Unfortunately, these actions were too little, too late. The
  advantage lies not only in doing the right thing, but in making the right move more quickly than rivals. On the strategic
  side, the power of being first is obvious. Legend seized significant market share with its Pentium-based PC, price cuts, and
  tailored products before Great Wall (or the Western PC firms)
  had a chance to respond. The advantage of speed also extends to operating improvements. The sooner a company
  rationalizes its production or cuts working capital, the sooner
  it reaps the resulting cash flow increases. Moreover, after
  completing one initiative successfully, executives can move on
  to the next priority. A slower rival, in contrast, will still be
  struggling to catch up with the last move as the more agile

company moves on to the next. Each time the faster company starts and completes a cycle of operating improvement, it gains an incremental advantage over the laggard.

- *Cumulative benefits.* A company that consistently outcycles its rivals can stockpile incremental advantages over time by seizing fleeting opportunities, managing threats, and increasing efficiency. The cumulative disparity can grow over time from a small gap into a gaping chasm. When a sudden-death threat emerges, the leader can weather the storm. When a golden opportunity comes along, the leader is strong enough to seize it.

    Successive iterations of the SAPE cycle confer another advantage. They allow the leading company to choose the timing of its actions. Legend, for example, built a significant advantage relative to Great Wall between 1993 and 1996 through a series of operational improvements. This allowed Legend to decide the optimal time to introduce new products and cut prices when competitors would find it difficult to respond. Legend could have cut prices or introduced new products earlier or waited until later, but it was its cumulative advantage that conferred the luxury of choice.

The Power of Priorities

Priority, as we use the term, refers to something that is more important than other considerations. Priorities can be actions, such as "build brand recognition" or "enter a new market." They can also be quantitative targets, such as "achieve profit" or "achieve sales objectives," that do not specify how to attain these goals. By setting a small number of key priorities (usually three to five) for a specific period of time, managers can use priorities to keep themselves and their organization focused on what is truly important based on their assessment of the situation. They can also use these priorities to guide resource allocation. Concretely, you can envision key priorities as a list of three to five things that the top executives of a company might hang on a piece of paper on a cork board behind their desks.

The SAPE Cycle
and the OODA Loop

THE SAPE CYCLE builds on a related model in military theory. Understanding the military antecedent can illuminate the business version. In the early 1970s, John Boyd, a colonel in the U.S. Air Force, began to study a question that had puzzled military observers for years.[7] During the Korean War, American fighter pilots had outgunned their enemies, who were flying Soviet-made MiGs, by a ratio of ten to one. This was puzzling because the Soviet MiGs were superior on traditional dimensions of performance: they climbed quicker, flew faster, and shot more accurately. Boyd discovered, however, that the American planes had two critical advantages. They had a bubble canopy that increased pilots' visibility relative to MiG flyers, who peered through a smaller window. The U.S. planes also benefited from better hydraulics, which allowed pilots to switch from one action to another much more quickly than the MiGs.

Based on their advantages in observing the situation (the bubble canopy) and in maneuvering, American pilots devised a strategy of quickly shifting direction during engagements. The enemy could respond, but more slowly. With each successive change in maneuvers, the American pilot would gain a slight additional advantage. Finally, the gap would become so large that the U.S. pilot would have a clear shot at the enemy.

Boyd later generalized his findings to other forms of conflict. He argued that all battles, whether in the air, on land, or at sea, consisted of two opponents cycling through four steps. Both opponents first *observe* the situation and, based on their data, *orient* themselves; they then *decide* on the appropriate response, and finally *act*. Both opponents then observe the results of their earlier actions, evaluate the changed circumstances, and start the process again. Boyd referred to this cycle as the observe-orient-decide-act

(OODA) loop. His critical insight was that combatants who consistently move through the OODA cycle more quickly and effectively than their enemy gain a tremendous advantage over time. By the time the slower enemy reacts, the quicker opponent has already moved on to a new maneuver. Although none of the individual moves was decisive, their cumulative effect created a gap that left the slower opponent vulnerable.

Of course, business is not war. Companies cooperate to create value and compete over its distribution. Moreover, executives are not pilots. A pilot can personally decide on the best action and implement it immediately. An executive, in contrast, must influence the behavior of hundreds or thousands of employees to respond to the new situation.

Despite the differences between war and business, the similarities between the SAPE cycle and the OODA loop are illuminating. Both processes are iterative and time competitive. The faster company makes an operational improvement, seizes an opportunity, or responds to a threat, and the slower rival emulates this move, but only after a lag. By the time the laggard catches up with the leader, the faster firm has already moved on to the next thing. Both processes are also cumulative. Victory generally accrues to the company that has accumulated the most small advantages over time. The leader emerges over time just a bit faster and better through a series of incremental maneuvers. Business journalists and management gurus focus on the big bets or blunders, grand strategies, or long-term visions. The reality is more complex. The true essence of competition is the cumulative effect of many iterations.

We use the phrase "3 to 5 on a 3-by-5." To be concrete, "3 to 5" refers to the key priorities, and "3-by-5" refers to the size of a standard index card in the United States. (See figure 4-2 for an exercise to take stock of your company's priorities and those of your focal competitor.)

FIGURE 4-2

3 to 5 on a 3-by-5

You can use this figure to assess whether you are clear about your company's present priorities. Without preparation, quickly list the top three to five priorities for your company and for your most relevant competitor. Ask other members of your management team to independently conduct the same exercise.

Your company	Primary competitor
1) 2) 3) 4) 5)	1) 2) 3) 4) 5)

Setting priorities is common sense. The problem in organizations, however, is translating common sense into common practice. Table 4-1 lists a series of common problems executives encounter when taking stock of their own company's (and rival's) priorities. We focus in particular on *priority creep*, a common problem that occurs when the number of priorities expands over time. Managers begin with a short list but keep adding to it as they face minor crises, unforeseen opportunities, and the host of distractions inherent in turbulent environments. Of course, changing priorities is critical as circumstances evolve. Priority creep, however, occurs when mangers add new items to their list without crossing off less important objectives, activities, or initiatives. This, in turn, defeats the entire point of 3 to 5 on a 3-by-5. The list becomes so comprehensive that it no longer serves to focus attention or guide resource allocation.

We believe that priorities are more effective than mission, vision, purpose, strategy, or just about any other management tool in translating situational awareness and anticipation into effective organizational action. A small set of clear priorities can focus and align the entire organization around the critical few things versus the mindless many. Priorities can serve as a quick screen to ensure that critical resources—particularly money and good personnel—are placed where

TABLE 4-1

Warning signals

After listing priorities for your company and your most relevant competitor, compare 3-by-5 index cards across your management team. Below are a few common warning signals of trouble.

- You don't know your priorities.
- You have more than five (priority creep).
- You have only one priority (too focused for an unpredictable environment).
- Your colleagues list different priorities.
- You do not know your competitor's priorities.
- Your company is consistently too little, too late, or too slow in executing on its priorities compared to rivals.

they can do the most good. In contrast to vague statements of mission, purpose, vision, or strategy, priorities are actionable. Managers can translate them into concrete objectives and targets that cascade down the entire organization.

Priorities are also time specific. They can and should change either when they are achieved (one of life's little pleasures is crossing a priority off the 3-by-5) or when unforeseen circumstances force a reordering. Contrast this with grander notions of vision, mission, purpose, or strategy, which often are assumed to last forever. The time-sensitive nature of priorities has another advantage. By setting deadlines for achievement of priorities, managers can maintain a sense of urgency and control the timing with which their company moves through the SAPE cycle. Vision, mission, and strategy, in contrast, tend to be open ended in terms of timing and therefore provide no sense of urgency or timing to the organization.

Priorities While Actively Waiting

When a company faces a golden opportunity or sudden-death threat, setting the appropriate priorities is obvious. Senior managers set the key priority to seize the golden opportunity or survive the sudden-death threat. We use the term *main effort* to describe a single priority that is essential for the company as a whole. Examples of golden opportunities as the main effort include launching a major new product (Legend's launch of Pentium-based PCs), entering a new market (Ting Hsin's noodle reentry into Taiwan), and integrating a major merger or acquisition. Responding to a sudden-death threat is the other obvious example of a main effort. When top executives declare a main effort, everyone in the organization must ensure that their own actions support this effort. This may require pulling cash or talented people from other uses to ensure the success of the main effort.

Even in the most turbulent environments, however, companies will frequently find themselves in periods of active waiting during which they face neither a golden opportunity nor a sudden-death threat. That was Legend's position during the summer of 2004. Setting the right priorities is a critical element—perhaps *the* critical element—of waiting actively during periods of relative calm. Priorities during these periods must help the company prepare for major events in the future, even if the precise nature, magnitude, and timing of those events are unclear.

But how can executives set priorities for opportunities and threats they cannot predict with certainty or precision? They can do so by focusing their attention on midterm priorities that provide a company direction over one to three years. Of course, short-term goals, such as sales and production quotas for the next quarter, are also important, but most managers need little guidance in managing this routine aspect of their business. We believe three types of midterm priorities are particularly important:

- *Build reserves of cash and general managers.* During periods of relative calm, managers can build a war chest of cash to be deployed when the firm faces a golden opportunity or sudden-death threat. Finance theory suggests that firms in well-functioning capital markets need not stockpile cash because investors and lenders will provide money rapidly to fund attractive opportunities or help a viable company weather a transient shock. In turbulent markets, however, the cost and availability of capital may vary sharply over time. Even in sophisticated capital markets, the availability of funding shifts over time. In 1998, U.S. venture capitalists threw money at Internet start-ups like drunken sailors on shore leave. By 2000, they awoke with a nasty hangover and nearly stopped investing altogether. Thus, there is no guarantee that firms will have access to funds when they need them to seize a golden opportunity or survive a sudden-death threat. Moreover, raising funds generally takes time, which can reduce firms' ability to quickly respond. In calms between the storms, companies can also invest in cultivating talented general managers who can later be deployed to respond to major threats or seize opportunities. Liu and Legend's senior management team, for example, observed Yang for a period of six years before allowing him to head the PC business, and gave him successively larger positions to help him develop as a general manager.

- *Continuously improve operations.* Managers can continuously improve efficiency. Strategy gurus sometimes dismiss efficiency as less important than the big strategic decisions. In a turbulent environment, however, operational excellence assumes strategic importance. Efficiency results in high margins, which allows firms to build war chests. Efficiency also increases a firm's ability to withstand a host of negative shocks. The benefits of operational efficiency may be marginal in stable environments where the possibility of sudden-death threats is remote. They are critical, however, in turbulent environments.

- *Identify and manage potential risks.* Based on their monitoring, managers can take a variety of steps to reduce the probability or cost of potential sudden-death threats before they occur rather than responding to them after they have grown to a full-fledged sudden-death threat. Common examples are partnering with other companies to share risk and diversifying operations.

Summary

This chapter introduced the SAPE process as an alternative to the established strategic planning exercises common in many companies. It illustrated its benefits using a comparison of Legend and Great Wall and provided some practical tools to manage priorities. Key insights from this chapter follow. The next chapter introduces the *flexible hierarchy* as an organizational form well suited for translating priorities into effective organizational action, illustrating this construct with the example of Haier.

- *The SAPE (sense-anticipate-prioritize-execute) cycle* is an alternative to the traditional strategic planning process. Following the SAPE cycle, managers *sense* the current circumstances to form a holistic mental map of the situation, *anticipate* emerging opportunities and threats, *prioritize* strategic actions and operational improvements, and *execute* against these priorities.

- *Advantages of the SAPE cycle* relative to traditional strategic planning processes include SAPE's explicitly iterative nature; flexible priorities based on changes in the competitive situation; incorporation of strategic decisions and operating improvements; focus on competition in time and timing; and integration of the cumulative benefits of iterative competition.

- At any point in time, managers should have a *small number of priorities* on which to focus their attention and the organization. Priorities shift over time in response to changing circumstances, but they are always limited in number and understood throughout the organization. They can be either operational or strategic, depending on the situation. Priorities are more important than vision or strategy in unpredictable markets.

- *"3 to 5 on a 3-by-5"* is a simple exercise managers can use to test the clarity of their priorities and understanding throughout the organization.

- *Priority creep* occurs when a short list of priorities slowly expands over time as managers add new items to their list without crossing off less important objectives, activities, or initiatives. A laundry list of priorities provides no focus or guidance regarding resource allocation decisions.

- A *main effort* is a single priority that is essential for the company as a whole at a point in time—usually either seizing a golden opportunity or surviving a sudden-death threat. All resource commitments and initiatives within the organization must be evaluated by how well they support the main effort.

- When a company faces neither golden opportunities nor sudden-death threats, its priorities should help the company actively prepare for major events in the future. These priorities include building reserves of cash and general managers, continuously improving operations, and managing potential risks.

FIVE

Develop a
Flexible Hierarchy

T HE PREVIOUS CHAPTER discussed how companies set (and reset) their priorities in response to a shifting situation. Selecting the right objectives is a necessary step for surviving and thriving in a turbulent environment, but it is far from sufficient. Managers must ensure that the entire organization can execute rapidly and effectively against chosen priorities. The SAPE cycle often breaks down between the prioritization and execution steps, with top executives declaring a clear set of priorities that the organization cannot execute quickly or effectively. Middle managers and employees dissipate energy on inconsequential activities, for example, or capital is tied up in projects or initiatives that do not support the main effort.

Returning to the metaphor of car racing, managers in fast-changing contexts must frequently shift gears, but often lose traction and stall during the shift. This risk is particularly acute in unpredictable markets where frequent shifts in the environment require regular rejiggering of priorities. The challenge is not recognizing that priorities are important—that is common sense. The real challenge is consistently executing, which is harder than it seems.

How can managers ensure consistent, effective, and rapid execution of priorities that change with shifts in the context? This broad challenge entails several more focused challenges: How can executives cascade priorities throughout the organization? How can the company balance centralization in setting priorities with decentralization in executing them? How can it develop and maintain a cadre of managers versatile enough to shift from one initiative to another as external circumstances and appropriate priorities change? How can top executives avoid complacency and sustain a sense of urgency even in periods of relative calm?

This chapter introduces the *flexible hierarchy* as an organizational form well suited to translating top-level priorities into organizational action. It illustrates the flexible hierarchy with the case of the Haier Group, headquartered in Qingdao.[1] Haier is today the leader in China's home appliance market. The story of Haier's rise is legendary in China, and it is the Chinese firm that Western readers are most likely to know something about. Most accounts of Haier's success, however, focus on the company's branding efforts, its diversification into multiple appliances through acquisitions, and its expansion into global markets. These are all fascinating topics, and we will touch on them while recounting Haier's history. Our principle focus, however, will be on how Haier illustrates a flexible hierarchy in action. The key to understanding this model lies not in any general concepts, but in the nitty-gritty details of how they are implemented in practice. As a result, we focus our attention on the fine-grained features of the Haier organizational model.

Higher and Haier

The Haier Group is China's largest home appliance manufacturer, with an approximately 30 percent market share of the Chinese market for white goods, the most valuable Chinese brand, and self-reported

FIGURE 5-1

Haier's self-reported revenues ($ millions)

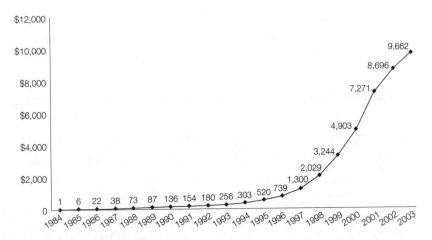

Source: Haier company documents.
The group revenues are based on unaudited company reports.

revenues of $9.7 billion in 2003.[2] Figure 5-1 plots Haier's historical revenues. Since the mid-1980s, the company has expanded its product range from refrigerators to a wide variety of white goods, including air conditioners, microwaves, and vacuums, as well as consumer electronics such as mobile phones and televisions. Haier exports to more than 150 countries globally and has twenty-two production facilities and eighteen design centers outside China. Worldwide, the company is ranked fifth among all appliance manufacturers and is second only to Whirlpool in refrigerator unit sales. In 2004, Haier ranked number one among the most admired global companies in China in a joint *Financial Times*/PricewaterhouseCoopers survey of more than one thousand CEOs from twenty countries.[3] CEO Ruimin Zhang has also gained international prominence. In 1999 the *Financial Times* ranked him twenty-sixth of the world's thirty most prestigious entrepreneurs, and in August 2003, *Fortune* magazine placed Zhang nineteenth among the twenty-five most powerful people in business outside the United States.[4]

The Foundation of Haier

Ruimin Zhang was born to a working-class family in Qingdao in 1949—the same year the People's Republic of China was founded. Zhang was a serious student who aspired to study Chinese classics in college. Indeed, his favorite readings include works by Confucius, Lao Tzu, and Sun Tzu. Zhang had the misfortune of graduating from high school during the Cultural Revolution, however, and could not pursue his dream of studying the classics at a university. Instead, he was required to work in a metal processing factory in Qingdao. Although he was forced into manual labor, Zhang's friends considered him lucky. As an only child, he was permitted to stay in his home province rather than being relocated to a remote rural area for reeducation by peasants.

For the next sixteen years, Zhang worked at the factory, ultimately progressing to the position of deputy director. Zhang felt deeply frustrated during these years by his inability to advance more quickly or introduce organizational innovations to improve the factory's operations. In 1984, an official from the Qingdao municipal government approached Zhang and offered him the chance to turn around the Qingdao General Refrigerator plant. A plum assignment this was not—three managers had already turned down the position as impossible. Zhang, however, was anxious to translate his organizational theories into practice and took the position.

The Qingdao General Refrigerator factory was originally founded in 1958 as a cooperative to repair and assemble electric appliances. In subsequent years the cooperative changed its name and product line several times to produce motors, instruments and meters, washing machines, and finally refrigerators. The succession of new products and name changes had failed to solve the cooperative's fundamental problems of poor product design, shoddy quality, and abysmal employee discipline: workers regularly urinated on the factory floor, and in winter, employees dismantled doors and window frames to take home for firewood. When Zhang took charge, he inherited a situation that was somewhere between bleak and desperate. Despite massive demand for home appliances, the company had difficulty selling its shoddy goods at a profit. In 1984 the company suffered a loss of over $635,000, well in excess of the book value of its assets, and resorted to borrowing from local farmers to meet its payroll.

Before taking his position, Zhang recruited three colleagues from the Qingdao municipal government to join his top management team, including Mianmian Yang, who joined as the chief engineer and deputy manager. None of the administrators in Zhang's bureau had enough work to keep them fully occupied, and most spent their time running personal errands or pursuing hobbies at work. In contrast, Yang—who had earned her engineering degree from the local polytechnic—spent her time reading edifying books. Yang had not only engineering talent but also practical work experience on the factory floor—a combination that proved invaluable later in instilling quality into Haier's processes.

Zhang and Yang complemented each other well, with Zhang focusing on strategy and relationships with the government, and Yang implementing methods to keep the operations running smoothly. Yang later described her most important managerial attribute as her tenacity quotient (TQ), that is, a tenacious persistence in achieving the company's priorities undeterred by the setbacks inevitable in the Chinese economy.

Building Quality: 1984 to 1991

With his team in place, Zhang took decisive steps to halt the factory's decline: he freed working capital, instilled workplace discipline, and introduced advanced technology and management practices from abroad. After Zhang's actions were carried out, many employees believed the company was sitting pretty. In the mid-1980s, booming demand for refrigerators outstripped supply. Customers often waited weeks or months before they could purchase home appliances, and some resorted to waiting outside factories in the hope of persuading factory managers to sell them products directly.

Because demand outstripped supply in the early 1980s, most competitors simply pumped out volume with little regard to quality or design. Zhang, however, anticipated that the market situation was set to change. Based on his interviews with customers and study of markets in developed countries, Zhang anticipated that the basis of competition would shift from quantity to quality once industry capacity caught up with demand. As customers grew more educated and enjoyed more choices, they would buy based on product quality. Zhang thus saw product quality as the company's top imperative going forward.

Zhang and Yang set a number of concrete priorities consistent with improving product quality, including achieving European product quality standards and Japanese process efficiency. In 1985, Zhang negotiated an agreement to license technology from the German appliance maker Liebherr to introduce world-class technology into the factory's product line. When Zhang and a colleague went to Beijing to secure the necessary government approvals, the bureaucrat in charge would not agree to see them because the factory was too small to warrant his attention. Zhang simply stood outside the building for hours in the middle of a blizzard until the official finally agreed to see him. Whereas other rivals rushed willy-nilly into other products, Zhang decided to delay diversification until Haier's refrigerators achieved European quality standards. Zhang and Yang also studied Japanese quality management techniques, translated these into concrete goals, and oversaw their implementation throughout the factory. The company turned away orders if the additional volume would force workers to cut corners on quality.

Despite this flurry of activities, Zhang was dissatisfied with the factory's progress on quality and decided to send a strong message. In 1985, a customer visited the factory to complain about a faulty refrigerator, and his search for a replacement product revealed further defective products. Zhang and Yang ordered a test of the factory's inventory and discovered seventy-six, functional but defective products. In the past, such appliances had been sold at a discount for cash or given to government officials as "gifts." Zhang, however, had the defective refrigerators lined up and labeled with their specific faults and the names of the workers who produced them. Zhang assembled the entire workforce to watch while the responsible employees were required to smash the faulty appliances with a sledgehammer.

Workers, many in tears, protested the destruction. After all, even a defective refrigerator at that time was worth nearly two years of a worker's salary. And in 1985, the company's cash flow position was still perilous. Zhang and Yang also docked themselves one month's pay as a penalty for allowing the production of defective refrigerators under their watch. The smashing of the seventy-six refrigerators was a defining moment in Haier's history and gave teeth to the commitment to quality. That commitment paid off. Only four years later, Haier won the top quality award in China and even surpassed the quality of its German partner.

In the late 1980s, China's appliance industry suffered from a sudden-death threat. Rapid growth in demand had attracted widespread entry by new domestic competitors, leading to overcapacity of undifferentiated products and brutal price wars. The late 1980s witnessed a shakeout among refrigerator producers. None of the four leading producers in the 1980s (i.e., Snowflake, Wan Bao, Xiang Xue Hai, and Shuanglu) remained among the top six a decade later. Haier's reputation for quality, however, allowed it not only to survive the shakeout but also to gain in share of units sold while holding and raising prices. The early commitment to quality allowed Haier to weather the sudden-death threat and emerge stronger than many of its rivals.

Growth Through Diversification: 1991 to 1998

By the early 1990s, Zhang and Yang had honed their factory's manufacturing processes to ensure consistent quality on par with global appliance makers' best products, and their Haier brand earned a reputation for outstanding quality throughout China. At this point, Zhang decided the time was ripe to diversify into other white goods in order to apply Haier's manufacturing know-how, nationwide distribution, and brand equity in related product areas. In 1991, Zhang took the first small step toward diversification by arranging the merger of the Qingdao General Refrigerator factory with two local factories—one making freezers and the other air conditioners. The combined entity was christened the Haier Group. The two factories did not add much to Haier's production capacity, however, and Zhang waited actively for the next opportunity.

Zhang did not have to wait long. Zhang frequently said that Chinese entrepreneurs require three eyes rather than two when spotting opportunities: one constantly monitoring the organization for new ways to unleash and harness employees' energy, the second trained on the customer to identify emerging needs, and the third observing the political-regulatory context for windows of opportunity. Zhang's third eye spotted a golden opportunity in spring 1992, when retired paramount leader Deng toured southern China exhorting his countrymen to experiment boldly while chastising those who dawdled toward reform. Based on Deng's words, Zhang anticipated that China was poised for widespread economic reform that would stimulate demand for a wide range of electric appliances. More urgently, he spotted a window of opportunity to raise growth capital, since an easy credit policy was consistent with Deng's policy.

In April 1992, Zhang secured a large loan from the Qingdao Industrial and Commercial Bank, and in June Haier acquired approximately 800 mu of land (over one-half million square meters) for a planned industrial park to design and produce multiple appliances. One month later, the People's Bank of China, China's central bank, issued an edict requiring banks to reduce lending to slow down the overheating economy, and dampen real estate speculation in particular. Had Zhang delayed only a few months, Haier would have missed the window to raise the funds for its industrial park. But he didn't. The company broke ground in November 1992 on what was to become China's largest research and production center. To generate cash flows quickly, Haier brought the production lines on line successively and worked with global joint venture partners for access to product and process technology. Haier partnered with Japan's Mitsubishi Heavy Industries, for example, in air conditioners and Italy's Merloni on washing machines.

By the time the initial phase of construction was completed in 1995, Haier's industrial park housed more than twenty-five production lines, which collectively had generated sufficient cash flow to repay nearly three-quarters of its initial loan. In November 1993 the Haier Group raised approximately $8 million to fund construction through an initial public offering on the Shanghai stock exchange of a subsidiary company, the Qingdao Refrigerator Company.[5]

Zhang recognized that many mergers failed in China when government officials arranged a shotgun marriage between a strong competitor—be it a collective enterprise or foreign multinational—and an ailing state-owned enterprise. The government hoped the strong company would prevent the weaker from drowning, but often the struggling operation dragged its counterpart under. To avoid a similar fate, Zhang decided to merge with companies with an excellent resource base—specifically, production lines, technology, and a young workforce—that lacked only the management expertise to leverage their assets. Zhang encapsulated this approach in the phrase "Capture the stunned fish, not the dead ones."

Zhang spotted a golden opportunity to catch a "stunned fish" through a merger with the Qingdao Red Star Electric Appliance Company. Red Star—a collective enterprise headquartered in the same city as Haier—had been one of the top three washing machine manufacturers in China but in the early 1990s suffered losses stemming from poor management (the founder was imprisoned in 1991 for misusing funds). By 1995, Red Star's debt had reached $15.8 million, and the municipal government brokered a merger. Zhang sent a team of executives to introduce Haier's management processes within Red Star. Haier's executives did not inject capital into Red Star, but instead overcame initial resistance to implant the Haier culture. Within three months of the acquisition, Red Star turned a profit.

Haier's success in transforming Red Star gained widespread media attention, and soon municipal governments from all corners of China courted Haier to turn around their own ailing enterprises. As a result, Haier could select from a large pool of "stunned fish" when making subsequent acquisitions. Haier quickly ramped up capacity and seized market share in the new markets it entered. By 1997 it was among the top three brands nationally in its major product lines of refrigerators (over 30 percent market share nationwide), freezers (42 percent market share), washing machines (28 percent share), and air conditioners (24 percent share). The company has subsequently expanded its product line beyond household appliances, or so-called white goods, to include such consumer electronics as televisions and mobile phone handsets (black goods).

Going Global: 1999 to the Present

By 1999, Haier offered a full product line and had carved out a leadership position in China's white goods market. Zhang turned his sights toward global expansion. Zhang believed that Haier could only become a truly global company by establishing its own brand in the sophisticated markets of Japan, Europe, and the United States. Competing head to head with established branded players in these markets, however, would be prohibitively expensive. Zhang decided to tackle the low end of leading markets through products such as dormitory refrigerators and wine coolers. He sought to gain a toehold in the supercompetitive European and U.S. markets and later seek opportunities to enter the mainstream product market.

Haier, however, has added a new twist to this well-established strategy. Rather than competing solely on price, Haier is attempting to win through product innovation at the low end of the market. Many established players reserve their innovation efforts for the mainstream market and let the low end languish with outdated products. Haier, in contrast, has elected to conduct customer research and new product development at the low end with vigor.[6] The company has established eighteen international product design centers in cities such as Los Angeles and Tokyo that are dedicated to intensive research at the low end of the market and supported by production facilities in the United States, Japan, and Italy.

These centers have developed some interesting innovations. One U.S. design team, for example, visited college dormitories to study how student consumers used their refrigerators. The research revealed that many students set two dorm fridges side by side and placed a plank across them, using them as makeshift desks in their cramped rooms. Based on their research, the team designed a collapsible table on the side of a refrigerator, which students could unfold and use as a desk. The functional refrigerator-desk combination has been a great hit with college students, and Haier is now the U.S. leader in the mini-refrigerator segment.

This attention to the low end of the market has provided other hits as well, including a freezer with a bottom drawer for easy access and a successful line of wine coolers. Zhang is betting that Haier can establish a reputation for product innovation and quality (rather than low price alone) at the low end, and then build on this foundation to expand its presence. In 2002, Haier's U.S. subsidiary booked revenue of $250 million, with most of its production manufactured in Haier's factory in South Carolina. In 2002, Haier acquired the former Greenwich Bank Building (at 36th and Broadway) in New York City, a landmark structure renowned for its Corinthian columns, which now serves as Haier's U.S. headquarters.

The Flexible Hierarchy

Haier is an impressive story on many dimensions, but we focus on the organizational design that allowed Zhang to translate priorities into action. Haier is an excellent example of an organizational form that we observed in many of the companies we studied: the flexible hierarchy. A *flexible hierarchy* is an organizational form in which top executives set top-down priorities for the organization, but allow middle managers and employees great latitude in negotiating their specific objectives and autonomy in executing against them. Zhang was active—indeed, nearly autocratic—in setting priorities, and in this regard Haier resembles a traditional hierarchy. On the other hand, managers and employees participated in setting their specific objectives and enjoyed wide latitude in *how* they achieved them. Haier is hierarchical in top-down prioritization, and flexible in execution.

The flexible hierarchy may seem like common sense, but in fact it conflicts with prevailing theories of the optimal organizational design for unpredictable markets.[7] These theories argue that companies in complex, dynamic, and interactive environments should adopt a highly decentralized organization composed of loosely coupled business units receiving minimum guidance from the top. Loosely coupled business units, according to this theory, can respond independently and quickly to shifts in their local environment without hindrance from a centralized authority.

A loose confederation of autonomous units, however, suffers from three limitations in unpredictable environments. First, a major threat or opportunity to an organization may fall between the cracks of established units or be too large for any one unit to tackle alone.[8] None of Haier's business units (e.g., refrigerators, washers, microwave ovens), for example, could have afforded by itself the investment in brand building, distribution, and manufacturing required to expand globally. Second, loosely coupled units may be reluctant to take resources from their existing uses to contribute to the main effort, whether through killing new product development, reducing head count or capacity, or losing key managers.[9] Reluctance to free up local resources can slow a firm's response to a sudden-death threat to the extent each division avoids required reductions in head count, capacity, and so forth while waiting for others to bite the bullet. Hoarding resources also prevents companies from pursuing golden opportunities if seizing them requires a concentration of resources to support the main effort.[10] Finally, although the independent units might ultimately agree on the best course of action, a time-consuming process to build consensus can prevent a company from seizing fleeting opportunities or responding to sudden-death threats in time to beat rivals through the SAPE cycle.

The key to the flexible hierarchy is its ability to translate priorities into action. There is, of course, nothing new about companies executing against priorities. The principle of managing by objective was first articulated over fifty years ago by Peter Drucker and was undoubtedly in practice decades or even centuries prior to entering the management lexicon.[11]

However, two challenges arise specific to executing against priorities in an unpredictable environment. The first is the need for speed. Recall the importance of time-competitive execution when trying to beat rivals through successive iterations of the SAPE cycle. Second, the specific priorities in unpredictable markets might change quite abruptly and dramatically. In Haier's relatively short history, priorities shifted from quality improvement efforts to rapidly securing funding, to building a new industrial park, to product-line diversification, to postmerger integration, and to global expansion that included setting up operations abroad (to mention only a few of the more prominent examples). The shifting nature of priorities contrasts with objectives in more stable environments, which are likely to entail incremental improvements on the same dimension—for example, steady quality improvement or incremental product-line extensions.

The secret to executing against shifting priorities rapidly and effectively does not lie in any great conceptual breakthrough. Rather, it depends on the practical steps companies take to ensure that they do not slip gears and stall between prioritization and execution. The remainder of this chapter illustrates some of the concrete steps that Haier takes to ensure that top-level priorities are translated into action throughout the organization.

Priority-Based Contracts

Performance agreements between managers and their direct reports are a key mechanism for giving priorities traction through all levels in the organization. Each year, Zhang and Yang decide on a small number of overarching priorities for the corporation as a whole, typically three to five. They discuss these with their direct reports in order to agree on tangible performance objectives for the year. Subsequently, these executives meet with their subordinates to agree on a small number of targets, and the process cascades down the organization all the way to plant floor employees.

The corporate priorities in this system are set by top management and are not subject to negotiation. As these priorities cascade down each level of the hierarchy, superiors negotiate with their subordinates to translate overarching priorities into specific objectives that their subordinates can achieve. These are genuine negotiations rather than a series of diktats imposed by the level above. Superiors clarify the overarching corporate priorities, explain their personal performance objectives, and negotiate concrete, measurable objectives for their subordinates. The subordinates play an active role in these negotiations, clarifying their understanding of corporate priorities, explaining the circumstances they face, negotiating achievable objectives, and specifying resources necessary to achieve their objectives. Finally, and most important, managers at every level grant their subordinates great discretion and autonomy in *how* they achieve the agreed-upon objectives. This process leaves no room for top-down micromanagement. Table 5-1 summarizes the roles of superiors and subordinates in these negotiations.

The agreements resulting from these negotiations resemble a legal contract between a manager and his or her subordinates in which the boss provides clarity on current priorities, required resources, and autonomy in execution in exchange for the subordinates' commitment to achieve performance targets. The company's overarching priorities provide the context for striking these bargains. The term *priority-based contracts* describes agreements between a manager and his or her subordinates to achieve agreed-upon objectives that are consistent with the company's overall priorities at a point in time.

Priority-based contracts are critical in unpredictable markets because they grant employees the autonomy to harness their in-depth understanding of local circumstances to select the best way to achieve

TABLE 5-1

Priority-based contract

Superior	Subordinate
Communicates rationale for priorities	Clarifies own understanding of rationale
Negotiates to translate priorities into concrete objectives for subordinate	Negotiates to translate priorities into concrete objectives for self
Provides resources necessary to achieve objectives	Identifies resources necessary to achieve objectives
Grants subordinate autonomy in execution	Enjoys great discretion in how to achieve objectives
Monitors execution against agreed objectives	Reports data on own performance against goals
Agrees to provide credit and recognition for achievement of objectives	

objectives, rather than forcing them to rely on some preordained set of steps or a distant manager's view of how to get things done.[12] By granting this autonomy, priority-based contracts can unleash the creativity and initiative of individuals throughout the organization. The tight linkage between overall corporate priorities and individual objectives ensures that this autonomy and initiative is channeled in the same direction throughout the organization.

Transparency in Monitoring Performance

Of course, most companies have some mechanism to translate corporate priorities into performance objectives. But few work as well as Haier's. In many companies, each employee's or manager's objectives and performance are guarded as jealously as state secrets. This secrecy often breeds distrust. Without clarity about individuals' objectives and performance, people speculate that promotions, demotions, and rewards result from office politics or personal connections rather than achievement. These conspiracy theories, in turn, erode people's trust in the system and their willingness to view their contracts as binding.

Haier, like other successful companies we studied, put objectives and performance in the public domain. This is not always easy, as Haier's managers discovered. After years of cronyism and opaque processes, employees in acquired companies viewed the Haier way with skepticism at best and cynicism at worst. Despite agreement on clear objectives and criteria, employees initially believed that only new employees or senior management's protégés would receive bonuses. Haier's transparency in posting objectives and monitoring performance quickly dispelled this skepticism.

When Haier manager Yongsen Chai took over as general manager of the newly acquired Red Star factory, for example, he publicly posted his own objectives for all to see, publicized current performance against goals, and fined himself (rather than his subordinates) when the subsidiary missed targets. Having set this example, it was easier for Chai to later penalize Red Star middle managers who failed to achieve their own objectives. Chai subsequently evaluated all managers based on their performance against goals on a weekly basis, generated a list of good and bad managers, and posted this evaluation publicly. Although managers initially resisted the public ranking, they ultimately grew accustomed to the system, which encouraged poorly performing employees to evaluate their errors and take responsibility for fixing them.

In 2000, Haier adopted an even more extreme form of performance posting, which it had observed while studying best practices among Japanese companies. Each manager or employee within a department is evaluated monthly on his or her performance against negotiated goals (most of which are quantitative). Managers and employees are then rank ordered relative to their peers, and the results of the rank ordering are publicly posted. Photographs of all the managers in an operating unit or staff function (e.g., marketing, human resources) are posted prominently, with their rank number for that month. Thus, a department with twenty managers would have twenty photos, each with a number between 1 and 20 affixed to his or her photograph. The best performers are marked with red smiling-face magnets to signify their accomplishment, the majority are marked with green magnets to denote they are on target, and the bottom few performers for the month bear yellow frowning faces to highlight that they are behind others in ranking. The performance of the company's top executives against their objectives is posted early each month outside the company cafeteria, with arrows denoting whether their performance is trending upward or downward relative to the preceding month.

By publicly posting objectives and performance, top executives increase the costs of failing to deliver on the contracts they agreed to with their superiors. They must live with the embarrassment (as well as other penalties described later) if they fail to meet their objectives. The public posting of all managers' objectives also reinforces the company's overall priorities. The constant public monitoring of ongoing results builds trust and a belief in the fairness of the system as a whole. Managers and employees may not enjoy the constant pressure of public evaluation, but they understand the rules of the game and appreciate that they are enforced consistently for everyone. In addition to transparency, the design of roles and responsibilities is critical to a flexible hierarchy's success. The system requires a continuous chain of responsibility, for example, as well as a clear definition of responsibility for each employee.[13]

High-Powered Incentives

The proper incentives give teeth to priority-based contracts by rewarding employees who achieve their objectives and by penalizing those who miss targets. Of course, all companies have some system for rewarding performance. In many companies, however, managers see a miniscule bonus—perhaps 5 percent to 7 percent of their base compensation—if they hit targets, but face no penalty for failure. Managers may not be promoted as fast as they had hoped, but there is little chance of being fired for missing targets. Many lower-level employees are excluded altogether from performance-based incentives. Not so at Haier, which uses the following system.

- *Share the financial upside.* Managers who deliver on their commitments reap significant rewards, including eligibility for promotions that are not open to their lower-performing peers. Starting in 1989, Haier made compensation of each employee 100 percent variable and linked to performance in meeting monthly market targets. The compensation of every employee—from factory worker to senior executive—follows the same basic formula. Basic salary (which is a function of seniority and previous achievement) is multiplied by the percentage of monthly target achieved. Losses attributable to the individual (such as defective products, inventory loss, and loss of accounts receivable) are then deducted from the adjusted salary. The employee's portion of gains from efficiency improvement and additional sales attributable to his or her actions are then added to calculate the final compensation. Haier employs sophisticated systems to track its employees' contributions to revenues, costs, working capital, and other drivers of the group's financial performance.

- *Share the credit*. Haier rewards employees by giving them credit for their innovations through a number of mechanisms, chiefly through public ceremonies that recognize outstanding contributions. One of the most coveted honors in Haier is having a new product named after the innovator. As of September 2003, there were over nine hundred process and product innovations named after employees throughout all Haier operations. For example, the president of Haier America, Michael Jemal, had an idea for a freezer that opened from the top for items stored high, but also included a drawer at the bottom for items lower in the freezer. The two compartments allowed both easier access to products either at the top or bottom as well as different temperatures in the two compartments. The product was launched in the Chinese and U.S. markets as the "Michael Freezer," with ads explaining its origins.

  Naming extends to process innovations as well. In any Haier factory, visitors will notice multiple process improvements named after the workers who developed them. Naming process innovations is virtually cost free, but it means a great deal to the honored employees. In a refrigerator factory, for example, one production step requires employees to punch holes in the refrigerator door. Visually inspecting the alignment of the holes was an awkward and time-consuming task that involved crawling on the floor and opening and closing the refrigerator door. An innovative employee, Yunyan Gao, placed a small mirror so workers could observe whether the holes had been punched correctly on both sides without having to move themselves or the door. This small step saved a great deal of time and labor, and the "Yunyan mirror" was rolled out throughout the factory.

- *Penalize underperformance*. Haier, of course, relies on sticks as well as carrots. Across departments, managers who consistently land at the bottom of their departmental rankings risk decreased salary and demotion. When Haier managers fail to meet their objectives, they are placed into one of three categories. Those with only minor improvement gaps are to be put on "medication" and receive on-the-job training to improve their skills. Managers with more serious performance shortfalls receive "intravenous injection"—more intensive supervision and demotion. Repeated and serious performance deficits lead to "hospitalization" and removal from their positions. In a typical year, as many as one-quarter of Haier's top managers were removed from their positions, demoted, or put on one-year probation. Demotions, as well as promotions, are published in the corporate newsletter.

These penalties extend to factory floor workers as well. Production workers are evaluated daily against their quantity and quality objectives. In the past, employees who fell short of expectations were forced to stand on a set of yellow footprints at the end of the working day and confess to their assembled coworkers that they had failed to meet their goals, analyze the source of failure, and explain to their workmates how they planned to improve the next day.

In an interesting twist, the practice of public confession of sins was changed when employees in Haier's U.S. factory threatened lawsuits if forced to step in the yellow footprints, citing diminished self-esteem and possible human rights violations. Managers at the U.S. subsidiary modified the footprint practice so that high performers stood in the footprints (now red) to share their success stories and good practices with workmates. Underperforming employees were given stuffed pink pigs, but not publicly taken to task. This new process worked so well that Haier imported the change to its Chinese factories, which now also rely on the red footprints of praise rather than the yellow footprints of shame.

Limit the Downside Risk of Decentralization

Many managers recoil at Haier's extreme level of decentralization because they fear the risks of devolving responsibility throughout the organization. Often this reasonable concern actually masks a deeper desire to retain power and an unwillingness to let go. That

said, decentralization does entail risks. Haier managed these risks in
a number of ways. The most obvious, of course, was tightly linking
the main effort to concrete objectives and cascading these throughout the organization. This process reduced the risk of employees losing focus on what was truly important. But that is not the only risk
management tool.

- *Set clear boundaries.* Although managers are given broad
  autonomy, top executives also provide strict boundaries that
  cannot be crossed. For example, at Haier, service and quality
  can never be compromised when trying to reduce costs or
  speed new product innovation.

- *Perform spot checks.* Because Haier has a data dashboard
  that provides fine-grained detail and a system of cascading
  objectives, senior management can perform periodic spot
  checks on variances against plan on real-time data. For example, the director in charge of Haier refrigerator products has
  real-time access to the daily sales of forty-two sales sub-
  sidiaries across the country. The systems will automatically
  rank these companies and show which company is not on
  track to meet its daily sales goals. The director can immediately contact sales manager to dig deeper into the situation
  and can allocate more resources if necessary. The existence of
  clear objectives and frequent updates of performance against
  these objectives allows senior executives to focus their scarce
  time and attention on targets that aren't being met.

- *Use incentives to capture both the downside and upside.* The
  structure of incentives plays an important role in managing
  risk. In many Western companies, middle managers and senior
  executives receive stock options that grant them the right to
  sell their stock at a specified price. If the stock price goes up,
  they are rewarded. Because they receive the options for free,
  however, they bear no cost if the stock price drops. This incentive structure encourages managers to take reckless actions that
  increase the odds of their options being in the money. Haier's
  managers, in contrast, share both the downside and upside.

Train a Cadre of General Managers

The most elegant process for translating priorities into objectives will fail without a cadre of managers who can thrive in such a system. At Haier these managers share a few basic characteristics: They honor their commitments and are willing to bear the downside risk because they crave the upside reward if they meet their targets. They are willing to take the initiative and enjoy autonomy in achieving their objectives. Most important, they are sufficiently broad in their skills and experience to shift from one assignment to another as corporate priorities shift. Haier could respond to sudden-death threats and seize golden opportunities in large part because it had a reserve of general managers who could move without a hiccup from building a new industrial park to entering new product lines, integrating a major acquisition, or opening a foreign subsidiary. In short, a flexible hierarchy depends on a reserve of true general managers—rather than functional experts—who can successfully execute against very different priorities. Haier takes several actions to build this cadre of general managers:

- *Formal training.* All of Haier's China-based senior executives (totaling more than seventy) take part in a weekly training session each Saturday morning. Executives bring their current challenges to these sessions and work in teams of five to ten managers to brainstorm solutions for each member's challenge. The teams mix executives from different functions, geographies, and business units. During the week, the executives experiment with proposed solutions and report the results to teammates the following Saturday. This team-based learning approach exposes managers to a broad range of problems faced by their colleagues and helps them develop a broad perspective on the Haier Group's overall operations. This integrated perspective, in turn, prepares managers to shift rapidly from one assignment to another.

  Executives' problem-focused sessions are supplemented with content training in areas such as quality, marketing, and finance. These courses are anything but theoretical. Faculty coaches provide tools and functional expertise and also help executives develop action plans to meet their objectives. Faculty have strong incentives to help their students succeed. Faculty members are rank ordered based on their students' performance in meeting business objectives, and their bonuses are linked to their students' business performance. Imagine the impact on management education if business school professors were paid based on their students' professional success.

- *Frequent job rotation.* Formal training is important, but the most important learning comes on the job. Haier invests heavily in on-the-job training by frequently rotating its managers through new positions. To ensure they are familiar with different aspects of the group's operations, senior executives on average change positions every three years (with a maximum of six years). Frequent job rotation is inefficient in the sense that managers cannot always fully leverage their functional skills and expertise as they would if they spent their entire career progressing through one function. This forgone efficiency is on balance an investment rather than a loss, however; in exchange, Haier gains flexibility among the management ranks. Job rotation also extends to frontline employees. One interesting innovation to develop flexible and multifunctional frontline employees is the "twenty-five-minute supervisor." In this method, the production line supervisor yields twenty-five minutes per day to one team member, who supervises the team for that period. During these twenty-five minutes, the designated team member monitors performance and responds to problems in every step of the process.

- *Cross-functional teams.* Serving on cross-functional teams also promotes general management skills. Haier's purchasing managers, for example, work in teams with representatives from product design, manufacturing, and logistics to manage not only the cost of buying raw materials such as steel but also the costs of carrying inventory, material-related defects, and shipping products. These costs are incorporated into purchasing managers' objectives, so they have a strong incentive to collaborate with colleagues from other functions to manage outlays. In addition to improving coordination, such interactions allow for better understanding of each other's functional areas. Through these interactions, managers enhance their understanding of the big picture, which eases their transition to new positions.

Keep the Pressure On

None of the companies we studied are comfortable places to work. The pressure is always on. Zhang captures this insight by comparing managing an organization to rolling a ball up a hill. Unless leaders apply constant pressure, the ball will roll down the hill. But Haier's very success can increase this gravitational pull. It is easy for employees to grow complacent, given Haier's historical success, size, and national prominence. But companies in unpredictable markets—like racers in the fog or armies during war—can never afford to let down their guard. One of the key challenges of managing a flexible hierarchy is maintaining constant pressure. This need is particularly acute in periods of relative calm, when the temptation is great to take a little longer or work a little less hard on operational improvements. Intel is one of the few high-technology companies to survive and thrive over decades of turbulence, and chairman Andy Grove sums up the reason in a single phrase: "Only the paranoid survive." So how can managers maintain the pressure, or paranoia if you prefer, in the wake of success and in relatively calm interludes?

- *Symbolic actions.* Managers can, of course, take symbolic actions that signal the importance of maintaining urgency. Zhang's smashing of the seventy-six defective refrigerators is one legendary example.

- *Setting ambitious targets.* The trick here is setting targets that are "almost" impossible, but not actually impossible. This is particularly difficult when an external sudden-death threat is not forcing higher targets.

- *Fostering internal competition.* The ordering by rank of executives described earlier serves to foster internal competition. Haier has developed other innovative ways to spur competition at different levels in the organization. In Haier's television assembly plant, for example, several production teams bid for new orders every week based on their track record in previous weeks. Even within the winning team, members may still lose their place to replacements from other teams if their individual performance does not meet the requirements of the team.

- *Job rotations.* Successful managers and employees can be forced to compete with their own past achievements through frequent job rotation. These moves force employees to prove themselves over and over again in new situations. This constant testing prevents managers and employees from settling into a smooth groove of incremental improvements in their area of functional expertise.

Summary

This chapter introduced the flexible hierarchy as an organizational form that enables companies such as Haier to execute quickly and effectively against corporate priorities, thereby completing the final step in the SAPE cycle. Important points are summarized in the following list. This chapter focused on the *internal* aspects of surviving and thriving in an unpredictable market. The next chapter looks outside the firm and discusses how companies manage the evolving relationships with customers, technology partners, suppliers, investors, and distributors required to survive and thrive in an unpredictable market.

- *Flexible hierarchy* refers to the organizational form that balances top-down priority setting with decentralized execution.

- *Priority-based contracts* are agreements between a manager and his or her subordinates to achieve agreed-upon objectives consistent with the overall priorities at a point in time. These cascade down the entire organization.

- *Transparency* requires executives to publicly post the objectives and performance of employees and managers. This transparency increases awareness of priorities and builds trust in the fairness and consistency of the system.

- *High-powered incentives* reward employees for meeting their objectives and punish them for failure. Nonfinancial rewards and punishments supplement monetary incentives.

- *General managers* with broad skills and experience are critical because they can shift from one position or assignment faster and more effectively than functional experts. Mechanisms to develop general managers include formal training, job rotation, and cross-functional teams.

- *Constant pressure* is required to keep the company from rolling down the hill into complacency. Mechanisms to maintain pressure include internal competition, symbolic actions, frequent job rotations, and ambitious targets.

SIX

Manage Relationships Dynamically

THE LAST CHAPTER focused on the *internal* aspects of a flexible hierarchy. This chapter turns its attention to the *external* relationships required to seize golden opportunities and avoid or manage sudden-death threats. Government agencies, customers, technology partners, suppliers, investors, and distributors provide the resources necessary to survive and thrive in an unpredictable environment. Success, therefore, requires managers and entrepreneurs not only to select good partners and craft solid deals but also, more important, to manage these external relationships as they evolve over time.

Working with partners rather than trying to do everything in-house confers several advantages in unpredictable markets: these relationships can minimize investment, parcel out risk, and allow a company to seize new opportunities and exit slowing businesses more quickly. They also have disadvantages, the most important being that dependence on these external parties can tie entrepreneurs' and managers' hands as they respond to changes in their competitive environment.[1] The relative balance of benefits and costs shifts over time, and entrepreneurs must manage these relationships as they evolve, a challenge we refer to as *managing relationships dynamically*. The appliance maker Guangdong Galanz has excelled at managing relationships in a turbulent environment, and its case study illustrates the costs and benefits of relationships, how these pros and cons shift over time, and, most important, how executives can manage them effectively in a constantly shifting context.

Guangdong Galanz: From Goose Feathers to Microwaves

Although not as well known as Haier, Guangdong Galanz has made impressive progress in the decade since it entered the white goods industry.[2] Galanz has carved out a commanding leadership position in the microwave oven sector. In 2003, microwave ovens accounted for only 4 percent of the total home appliance market in China. The Galanz brand dominates this niche, however, with the leading market share in every major Chinese city where it competes, outselling the second-largest brand (which varies by city) by a multiple of two to six times unit volume.[3] In Beijing, for example, Galanz enjoyed a 61 percent share of market (by revenues) versus 11 percent for number two LG; in Shanghai, Galanz had 46 percent versus 11 percent for SMC; and in Guangzhou, 42 percent compared with number two Midea's 8 percent. By way of comparison, Haier—the number one player in the larger air conditioner segment—had a 24 percent share of total industry revenues that same year.

Galanz has successfully defended its leadership position in the domestic market despite fierce attacks from aggressive new rivals Tianjin-LG, which entered in 1996, and Midea, which began selling microwaves three years later. Today, the company has over twenty thousand employees and is one of the largest home appliance manufacturers in China, with 2003 revenues of $1.3 billion.

Galanz built upon its position in China to become the global leader in unit production of microwave ovens, with annual output exceeding 16 million units in 2003. Galanz estimates that its share of global microwave oven unit production was over 40 percent in 2003, with its share in certain emerging markets in South America and Africa exceeding 70 percent of units sold. The vast majority of these units are manufactured for sale under other companies' brands. In 2001, the company diversified into air conditioner production, and within two years entered the ranks of China's top four exporters of air conditioners. Galanz executives have announced their goals of increasing annual air conditioner production volume to 7 million units in 2005 and at least 12 million units by 2008, and becoming the world's number one producer of air conditioners.

Qingde Leung and the Early Years of Guangdong Galanz

Guangdong Galanz today looks nothing like its original incarnation as the Guizhou Down Product Factory, a collective enterprise founded in 1978 to produce and supply goose down on an outsourced basis for branded clothing companies such as Yves St. Laurent. The collective enterprise was based in the Guizhou township of Shunde city in the Guangdong province, a township located at the Pearl River Delta and bordering Hong Kong. In the mid-1970s, Guangdong was considered a bit of an industrial backwater, with most of the country's heavy industry and technology concentrated farther north in the Beijing-Tianjin area and in Shanghai, among others. The provinces surrounding the Pearl River Delta, in contrast, were largely rural and lacked both up-to-date industrial equipment and the capital to acquire it.

All this changed in 1978, when the Communist Party announced its intention to create Special Economic Zones (SEZs) to experiment with free market reforms and with opening up to international markets. Suddenly, Guangdong, with its three SEZs of Shenzhen, Zhuhai, and Shantou, was on the front line of China's integration into the global economy. Qingde Leung was anxious to seize the moment. The southern entrepreneurs who pioneered capitalism are legendary in Chinese business circles, but Leung stands out even among them for his vision, diligence, and ability to survive the vicissitudes of a quarter century of turbulence.

Leung, who was born on a farm in 1937, first distinguished himself by completing high school, whereas most of his rural classmates dropped out before graduation to work the land. From 1956 to 1978, Leung enjoyed a varied career in a host of local state-owned enterprises, including the local distribution cooperative (the exclusive distribution channel under the planned economy), as well as management positions in a workshop of a steel mill, a printing factory, and an arts and crafts shop. In 1978, Leung—then a 42-year-old administrator in Guizhou township's industrial bureau—proposed that the town's party council set up a collective enterprise to wash and process goose feathers. The proposal met with stiff resistance, with one colleague vowing to crawl to the nearby Xijiao River if Leung succeeded in building the plant. Leung's proposal won approval by a narrow margin of the party council, but his colleague failed to make good on his pledge when eventually the plant was built.

In late September 1978, Leung and ten coworkers broke ground for the new factory on a deserted piece of land on the Xijiao River. Most groundbreakings are ceremonial affairs, where top executives dig the first shovelful of dirt and then go back to the office. Leung, in contrast, kept digging. The collective enterprise had only raised one-third of the approximately $400,000 required to build the plant, and the managers were forced to do the basic construction work themselves to conserve funds. With additional government bureaucrats dispatched to help, Leung completed the plant in seven months. By the summer of 1979, the facility employed approximately one hundred workers, who washed and processed feathers by hand for sale abroad.

Under Leung's leadership, the collective enterprise prospered. It backward integrated into poultry trading and expanded into related products, including woolen cloth. In 1985 it changed its name to the Guizhou Livestock Products Industrial Company to reflect its expanded business model. By 1992, the enterprise booked revenues of approximately $19 million and was ranked among the one hundred most successful township and village enterprises in China by the Ministry of Agriculture.

Golden Opportunity in the Domestic Microwave Oven Market

By the early 1990s, however, Leung anticipated that intense competition would depress profits in the textiles business, and he began actively waiting for the next golden opportunity. The local government proposed entering the synthetic fiber market, but Leung passed on the opportunity (a fortunate decision, since the business went bankrupt after the township entered later). On a business trip to Tokyo in 1991, Leung saw his first microwave oven and decided to add it to the list of possible opportunities. Although the enterprise had no expertise in white goods, the headquarters city of Shunde was rapidly emerging as China's manufacturing center for appliances and served as the headquarters for market leaders across several segments, including Rongsheng (refrigerators), Huabao (air conditioners), Aide (electric rice cookers), SMC (microwave ovens), Midea (electric fans), and a dense concentration of specialized components suppliers.

Leung sensed that domestic demand for microwaves was poised to take off. Although microwaves had been produced in China for more than a decade, most were exported. After conducting extensive research on the domestic market, Leung's team learned that microwaves were considered a luxury good, sold for $500 to $700 per unit, and that the miniscule household penetration rate in China was much lower than the 40 percent to 80 percent typical in Japan, Europe, and the United States. Moreover, no established competitor dominated the fledgling Chinese market. During this time period, many Japanese players, including Matsushita, Sharp, and Mitsubishi, started to set up joint ventures in China to produce microwave ovens for export.

Leung was not, of course, the only entrepreneur to notice the microwave oven opportunity. Between 1990 and 1998, over a hundred domestic firms began producing microwave ovens, including Haier, Sanle, Anlubao, and SMC.[4] Other foreign electrical appliance leaders—including Whirlpool, LG, and Samsung—also entered the Chinese market through joint ventures, bringing their expertise in branding, product technology, and global manufacturing scale and processes.

Leung, however, entered earlier than most new rivals. Many of the entries occurred in the mid-1990s: in 1996 alone eighty-eight new firms entered China's domestic microwave oven market. Haier and Midea were relatively late comers, entering the market in 1995 and 1999, respectively, and Whirlpool made its big move in 1995 when it acquired 65 percent of Shunde-based SMC, which had carved out an early leadership position in the small market. Later Whirlpool acquired the remaining 35 percent and made SMC its 100 percent subsidiary.

In June 1992, the Guizhou Livestock Products Industrial Company officially changed its name to the Galanz Group of Guangdong to mark its transformation into a microwave oven company. The name Galanz is modified from a Greek word meaning "magnificence." To develop the expertise required for microwave production, Leung visited Shanghai to persuade microwave oven experts to join his new venture. He finally succeeded in recruiting a few engineers from the Shanghai Eighteenth Radio Factory to work initially on a part-time basis as consultants. Among them was Rongfa Lu, who subsequently rose to be deputy general manager of Galanz. The newly formed team licensed technology from Toshiba in 1992 to produce a trial run of ten thousand microwave ovens in 1993 under the Galanz brand.

Lacking funds for a national launch, Galanz initially focused on the Shanghai market and got its big break when the Shanghai No. 1 Department Store (then one of China's largest department stores) agreed to stock the Galanz microwave ovens on a trial basis. Galanz's senior sales executive agreed to remove the microwaves if none sold in the first three days, and parked himself in the store to personally sell the ovens. Rivals disparaged Galanz's move from livestock to electronics, predicting the company would quickly go out of business. Leung posted these remarks on a bulletin board in the center of the microwave factory, gathered the workers to read them aloud, and challenged them to help him remove the board. Leung also placed domestic microwave leader (and cross-town rival) SMC squarely in the company's cross-hairs as its focal competitor. Galanz defied its critics, and the company sold 80 percent of its trial production run in Shanghai in 1993.

Galanz quickly built on its success in Shanghai to roll its products out nationally. To stimulate demand for microwaves, the company launched a national marketing campaign in 1995, placing advertisements and articles in over 150 newspapers and magazines to educate consumers on the benefits of microwave ovens; these marketing materials included practical cooking techniques and recipes. Galanz faced not only the normal setbacks encountered by any start-up, but also challenges of nearly biblical proportions. In June 1994, the Xijiao River experienced a flood reputed to be the largest in a century. The flood, which lasted two weeks, initially submerged the factory under eight feet of water; when it receded, it left more than a foot of mud in its wake. When he encountered weeping employees, Leung offered to pay the salary and traveling expenses of any employee who wanted to quit, but none took him up on his offer. Instead, Leung mobilized the remaining troops; within three days Galanz had resumed limited production, and it hit capacity three months later. Despite the flood, the company achieved sales of approximately 100,000 units and rose to second place in the domestic market for microwaves.

Galanz also had to overcome organizational challenges. In the early 1990s, Galanz was still owned 100 percent by the township government. Government policy, however, dictated that the ownership shift to a hybrid form in which the township would own approximately one-third of the enterprise (a share that would decline over time), while managers would own the remaining stake. Leung, himself a senior member of the local Communist Party, initially discounted ownership restructuring as a distraction from winning in the marketplace. Early in 1994, however, Leung had a change of heart and offered stock to management, and over sixty senior managers ended up with a 70 percent stake in the company. The outcome of Galanz's transition from goose feathers to microwaves was far from clear at this time, and many eligible managers declined the offered shares. To demonstrate his confidence in the venture, Leung took a personal loan and acquired all the unclaimed shares. As Galanz's prospects began to look up, Leung sold his shares (at a sharp discount to their estimated value) to other managers to share the wealth. The Galanz restructuring resulted in a broad base of middle managers with a substantial stake in the company's success and stood in contrast with many other ownership transitions that left a chairman owning the vast majority of a company.

In 1995, the company seized approximately 25 percent of the domestic market and overtook then-leader SMC. Few would have predicted this turn of events, since 1995 was the very year that SMC entered into a joint venture with the global appliance heavyweight Whirlpool, which was then making an aggressive foray into China. The joint venture initially provided an opportunity for Galanz, however, because Whirlpool inserted its own management team, that lacked local knowledge, dismantled SMC's experienced sales team, and required that major decisions be cleared first through regional headquarters in Hong Kong and then through the corporate office in Benton Harbor, Michigan. These changes slowed Whirlpool/SMC's ability to respond, and Galanz seized the initiative through a series of aggressive price cuts (of up to 40 percent each) and rapid-fire new product introductions that forced the joint venture to its knees and pushed many smaller competitors out of the industry altogether.

By 1998, Galanz had seized over half of the domestic microwave oven market. The price reductions led by Galanz lowered the average retail price of a microwave oven by nearly an order of magnitude within a few years, contributing to widespread consumer adoption that grew the market from a few hundred thousand units per year in the early 1990s to approximately 7 million units annually by the end of the decade.[5] Galanz benefited from a virtuous circle in which higher production volume produced economies of scale, which enabled further price cuts to gain more share. The company also invested over $200 million in research and development between 2001 and 2003, after establishing microwave research centers in China and the United States in 1997. Although Galanz has seen its domestic market share erode somewhat in recent years, it has successfully repelled attempts by other multinationals to unseat it from leadership in the Chinese market, including the aggressive foray by Tianjin-LG to compete on price while leveraging LG's brand and technology. Even the overall white goods leader, Haier, has been unable to win more than a token share of the microwave market to date.

Establishing Global Market Share Leadership

After securing its leadership with the Galanz-branded microwave in the domestic market by 1995, Galanz seized a golden opportunity to expand globally. During the Asian financial crisis beginning in the summer of 1997, South Korean microwave oven manufacturers, including Samsung and LG, were accused of dumping products in Europe, and local competitors petitioned for an antidumping investigation. While the European Union inquiry dragged on, most European microwave producers found themselves unable to compete with their Korean competitors on price, and the European manufacturers explored options to salvage their microwave business in the face of low-price competition from Korea.

The European companies' sudden-death threat was Galanz's golden opportunity. Yaochang Yu, Galanz's deputy general manager, later recalled how Galanz managers seized the opportunity: "We visited European manufacturers and asked how much it cost them to make a microwave oven. When they said $100, we explained that we could make them for half the cost at the same quality. And we had a deal." Galanz executives pioneered a novel partnership agreement in which European white goods companies would move their entire production lines to Shunde, where Galanz would make the microwaves for export back to their home markets for sale under the European companies' brands.

The partnership was compelling for the Europeans because they could more fully utilize their state-of-the-art production equipment. Factories in France, for example, typically ran only one shift per day, four days a week at that time, whereas Galanz ran three shifts daily seven days a week. The Europeans could also take advantage of China's low labor cost and Galanz's established expertise at efficient manufacturing processes and supply chain management. Because Galanz limited most of its branded sales to China, it did not compete with its original equipment manufacturer (OEM) partners on their home turf. This partnership was also a great deal for Galanz, which achieved economies of scale in manufacturing and purchasing. Galanz also secured permission to use its partners' manufacturing equipment to produce its own branded products for sale in China. In contrast to Haier, Galanz avoided expensive investments in building a global brand and distribution network.

Galanz rapidly extended its partnership model to over two hundred multinational partners and expanded its microwave production from approximately 1 million units in 1996 to over 12 million five years later. The company has subsequently extended its business model to other products, such as rice cookers and electric magnetic ovens, and has stated its ambition to move into the global air conditioner market.

Managing Relationships Dynamically

Galanz owes some of its success to Leung's sophistication in structuring deals with technology providers, distributors, and OEM customers. More important, however, was Galanz managers' ability to manage these relationships as they evolved over time. Of course, a moment's reflection clarifies that all companies must rely on relationships with stakeholders that contribute necessary resources, including capital, technology, and expertise. In stable markets, these relationships often slip into the taken-for-granted background, and managers passively sustain them without giving them much active thought. Firestone Tire & Rubber, for example, maintained tight ties with Ford Motor Company for nearly a century despite the automaker's continuous requirements for massive capital investment, hardball negotiations on price, and tendency to shift product liability to its tire supplier (recall the Ford Explorer recall).[6]

In unpredictable markets, entrepreneurs and executives cannot afford to take long-standing partnerships for granted, but must consciously reevaluate their shifting benefits and costs and actively manage them in light of shifting circumstances. An ancient Chinese proverb states that "there are no eternal friends and no eternal enemies, only interests." In an unpredictable market, moreover, these interests can shift substantially, often in a relatively short period of time. The absence of eternal friends and eternal enemies is important to remember in a fast-changing environment. Galanz stands out among its Chinese peers in managing relationships. It is important to note that Western managers have not cracked the code for managing dynamic relationships systematically. Companies in unpredictable markets such as information technology, medical devices, and tele-communications equipment are currently struggling to manage their relationships more effectively. The nascent business development function, for example, hardly existed a decade ago but now repre-sents a prominent way that companies in unpredictable industries attempt to manage their partnerships more systematically.[7] The fol-lowing sections provide some practical tips for managing relation-ships in dynamic markets.

Clarify the Costs and Benefits of Relationships

The first step in actively managing relationships is to assess their advantages and disadvantages. This may sound like Business 101, but a surprising number of companies trip up here. At one extreme they rush willy-nilly into countless deals with anyone that will say yes, and then lack the resources to make any of these deals work. The resulting partnership ends up as little more than a press release and a puff of smoke. At the other extreme, many Chinese companies try to do everything themselves, relying only on the local government for help. This do-it-yourself approach limits their options while spreading capital and management attention too thinly across multi-ple activities. Managers should clearly understand the pros and cons of key relationships.

Some questions for assessing relationships are as follows:

- *Which specific resources does this relationship provide to pursue an opportunity?* Often, individual entrepreneurs identify an opportunity but lack any resources to pursue it, or a resource-rich company spots a market gap but lacks the specific resources required to fill the gap.[8] For example, Galanz's experience in textiles provided no advantage in the microwave oven market other than the cash reserves it had accumulated. Instead, Leung and his executives had to assemble the required resources from scratch. They identified precisely which resources they needed and systematically searched for them: Leung targeted Shanghai's Eighteenth Radio Factory for technical and sales executives, Toshiba for product technology and manufacturing equipment, and Shanghai's leading department store for shelf space.

- *Does this partnership minimize investment?* Even when companies have the resources to pursue an opportunity on their own, it is not always in their best interests to put all of their eggs in that basket. Using partners' resources allows a company to preserve its capital. Galanz, for example, avoided capital expenditure to serve its OEM customers by using their equipment. The company went one step further, however, and also used its partners' equipment to produce Galanz brand microwaves. Making these smaller bets frees chips to spread across multiple experiments. Galanz used a portion of the money it saved on microwave oven production equipment to enter the air conditioner market.

- *Can this partnership accelerate entry?* Entrepreneurs and managers can generally secure the use of necessary resources through partnerships much faster than they can build them from scratch. When microwave market leader SMC entered into a joint venture with Whirlpool in 1995, Leung recognized that management turmoil at SMC/Whirlpool would not last forever. He and his team quickly forged partnerships with regional sales agents to aggressively push Galanz products through the window of opportunity before it shut as Whirlpool/SMC put their house in order.

- *Can this partnership accelerate exit (if necessary)?* External networks can not only speed entry, but also exit. Executives too often view internally developed projects as sacred cows that can never be slaughtered because the company has invested so much in them. A networked approach, in contrast, can foster agility in getting out of established businesses. Galanz's exit from the textiles business, for example, was accelerated by its reliance on a network of subcontractors and suppliers; ceasing operations did not entail major internal disruption but rather letting contracts with partners expire.

- *What risks does this partner share?* One of the main advantages of partnering is the ability to carve up risk and transfer it to the party best able to bear it. Historically Galanz, for example, has carried no finished-products inventory on its books. The company required dealers to pay cash on delivery for products and bear the inventory and accounts receivable risk. But it is critical to clearly specify the risks borne by each party. For example, when Galanz made a series of deep price cuts to stimulate consumer adoption, it risked hurting its distributors. Distributors might buy microwaves at a wholesale price of $100, for instance, and then end up carrying expensive inventory if Galanz cut prices to $60 later that week. Galanz mitigated this risk by agreeing to reimburse distributors for any loss in inventory value that resulted from a Galanz price cut. Partnerships can be a powerful risk management tool if the allocation of risk is clearly agreed upon and formalized between the parties.

- *Has this relationship become a shackle?* For all their benefits, relationships with external partners impose costs as well. Companies come to depend upon their partners for resources. This dependence, in turn, can put them at the mercy of their partners. Dependency is fine as long as partners' interests are aligned. Interests, however, tend to diverge over time, and these shifts can take place quite abruptly in a volatile environment. To paraphrase a Chinese proverb, a couple can share the same bed and same dreams when they fall asleep, but their dreams may diverge as the night wears on. In these situations, a powerful resource provider can prevent a company from responding effectively to shifts in the market.[9] Recall the case of Great Wall—the early leader in personal computers that lost out to Legend. Initially, Great Wall's close relationship with the Ministry of Electronic Industries (MEI) provided production licenses, funding, and access to technology. Over time, however, the MEI's demand for domestic content forced Great Wall to use substandard components, which hurt the company's reputation for quality.

Integrate Relationships into the SAPE Cycle

Given how the benefits and costs of relationships shift over time, managers cannot afford to let relationships run on autopilot. Rather, managers should monitor key partnerships, anticipate how the mix of costs and benefits is likely to evolve, shift priorities to ensure that benefits continue to outweigh costs, and execute quickly and effectively against concrete objectives for the partnerships. External relationships, in other words, are every bit as important in the SAPE cycle as changes in technology or macroeconomic conditions.

The evolution of Galanz's relationship with its distributors illustrates the power of integrating partnerships into the SAPE cycle. In the early 1990s, Galanz had multiple distributors in each region. These distributors specialized by product lines, with one dealer selling top-of-the-line microwaves in Qingdao, another distributing mid-range products in the same city, and a third moving inexpensive units. This distribution structure served Galanz well during its period of rapid growth because the extensive dealer network served first and foremost as a channel to get products into retailers' hands. While their wholesalers oversaw distribution and inventory management, Galanz executives were free to focus their efforts on advertising, brand building, and educating customers about the wonders of microwave ovens.

The situation shifted, however, a few years later, as the explosive growth in consumer adoption began to level off and Galanz was emerging as the market share leader. At this point, Galanz managers anticipated that the distinctions between high-, mid-, and low-end products would blur and that distributors in the same city would enter into cutthroat competition across the product tiers. Moreover,

Galanz executives anticipated a more active role for distributors in marketing the products locally and providing value-added services to retailers to differentiate Galanz products with enhanced service. In response to these shifts, Galanz made restructuring its distribution network a top priority for the company. Galanz cut the total number of distributors to facilitate closer cooperation on local marketing and service to retailers, and assigned an exclusive geographic license to one dealer per region to sell products across the tiers. Dealers were selected from many applicants based on their willingness to collaborate with Galanz in joint marketing and service provision.

Commit to Stretch Relationships

Galanz, like most of the successful companies we studied, entered into *stretch relationships*, or links with world-class partners that expose executives to best practices and force a company to approach this high level of performance itself.[10] Sophisticated partners place "unreasonable" demands on the organization and are generally a pain in the neck to deal with. They demand data and transparency, impose high standards, and push for constant improvement. It is much easier to settle for working with less demanding—often local—collaborators. What executives fail to recognize, however, is that these unreasonable demands are actually stretch partners' most valuable contribution to the firm's development. By actively seeking out and locking their organizations into stretch relationships, managers can pull their companies out of second-rate practices and drag their organizations—often kicking and screaming—to world-class practices and performance levels.

Although stretch relationships are sometimes painful, they can help companies close the gap with global leaders in their industry. In fact, we believe the Chinese companies that are most likely to emerge as formidable global competitors will generally not be state-owned enterprises that struggle to maintain cozy relationships with government ministries.[11] Rather, the most successful firms will be those, like Galanz, that enter into and successfully manage partnerships with sophisticated investors, customers, and technology suppliers. When

Leung decided to pursue the microwave oven opportunity, he did not select the most approachable competitor for technology. Rather, Galanz selected Toshiba as a partner because that Japanese company offered cutting-edge product and process technology. Subsequently, Galanz has moved to the frontier of the microwave oven technology globally through its stretch relationships with high-end original equipment manufacturers in the world's most demanding markets, including Japan, Europe, and the United States.

Many Chinese companies fall short, however, in forging stretch relationships with sophisticated capital providers, and it is worth pausing to explore this failure in more detail. Most Chinese entrepreneurs we spoke to saw global investors or banks as either sources of easy money in periods of irrational exuberance or troublemakers to avoid at all costs. In general, these managers preferred to raise capital from the easiest source they could—retained earnings and informal capital cooperatives, as well as Chinese banks and local stock markets. Like South Korean chaebol and Japanese keiretsu businesses before them, many Chinese companies, especially state-owned ones, have obtained these loans through a process that was as political as it was economic.

But stretch relationships with sophisticated capital providers can offer important advantages. The exceptional companies we studied that did seek out global capital providers, such as Sina or UTStarcom, illustrate these advantages. The obvious benefit, of course, is access to lower-cost capital. But there are less apparent benefits as well. Sophisticated venture capitalists, private equity firms, multinational banks, or institutional investors provide an external perspective on how the company is doing that serves as an excellent check and balance on management's internal assessment. Changes in credit ratings and shifts in stock prices, for example, provide early warning signs of potential threats or opportunities as perceived by people with their money at risk.[12] Stretch relationships with sophisticated capital providers can also provide external pressure for change and guidance on how to make those changes. Recall, for instance, how Sina's Zhidong Wang relied on venture capitalists to help identify constraints on scaling the company and also for guidance on overcoming these constraints.

Commit to Transparency

Forging and maintaining stretch relationships often requires an increased level of transparency. Managers must entice stretch partners to work with them, and one powerful means of doing so is to increase their level of transparency. Indeed, companies that aspire to emulate Galanz and partner with world-class firms generally have no choice but to become more transparent. This assertion may surprise some readers, both Chinese and Western, who believe that success in China's market depends on access to privileged information and *guanxi* (connections) with powerful people—the opposite of transparency.

Understanding the political situation is critical in countries such as China (or India, Russia, or Brazil, for that matter) that are undergoing fundamental political changes as they integrate into the global economy. Connections to policy makers matter in China, particularly to the extent they provide early warning of likely regulatory changes or, better yet, solicit executives' input in helping to shape these emerging policies. Of course, that is equally true in any other country in the world where government policy influences an industry. (If you doubt that, try landing a defense contract in the United States or running a large bank in France without political connections.)

The forces that are inexorably forcing global competitiveness are also pushing for greater transparency. The argument is simple. Entering into stretch relationships with customers, technology partners, investors, and suppliers enhances Chinese firms' ability to survive and thrive in turbulent markets. But these sophisticated partners often demand a high level of transparency before they will do business: Venture capitalists or global banks demand to see the financials before (and after) investing. Customers such as Ford or BMW insist on monitoring their suppliers' quality, production costs, and inventory to manage their own supply chain. Technology leaders such as Cisco or IBM demand visibility into their partners' development plans and performance in exchange for paying development costs or transferring technologies. Professional managers are more likely to leave a multinational to join a transparent Chinese company than an opaque one.

Lessons from Brazil

WHEN CHINESE MANAGERS look for best practices, they typically turn to the United States, Japan, or Western Europe. To understand how to become more transparent in an opaque environment, however, it is more instructive to study how companies achieved this goal in other low-transparency countries. A study of successful Brazilian firms identified a series of innovative steps that firms used to increase transparency beyond the legal requirements or norms of their local peers.[13]

Open Up the Books

From its inception, the Brazilian construction engineering firm Promon was employee owned. This choice of organizational form required Promon to disclose all of its transactions to its shareholders, more than five hundred partners in total. Many executives might see this requirement as a burden, but Promon's senior partners actually saw it as a source of competitive advantage. Promon's partnership structure allowed the company to insulate itself from government corruption. One senior Promon executive recalled:

> I remember a time when we received a visit from a distinguished gentleman who represented a senior government official. He asked us to please contribute 10 percent of all the work we were doing for the government to a special secret fund. I told him that we simply could not. Being an employee-owned company we would be unable to hide such a transaction. To my surprise, he understood and even sympathized with our values. Not only did we not lose any government contracts after that event, but this same gentleman referred business to us because we were trustworthy.

Promon's reputation for professionalism and honesty consistently attracted customers and partners. In 1993, for example, when Northern Telecom (Nortel) was looking for a local partner, it came directly to Promon because it had been burnt by a previous relationship with a Brazilian company and was looking for a company it could trust.

Report More Information Than the Capital Markets Require

Brazilian banking leader Itaú has benefited from its commitment to transparency in the capital markets. In 2001, Itaú voluntarily joined Level 1 reporting in the São Paulo Stock Exchange Governance Index, thereby committing to greater reporting than it was required to do by law. That same year, it began trading its American depository receipts on the New York Stock Exchange. The company has won a series of awards for its reporting and investor relations, including one from the Board of Governors of the U.S. Federal Reserve Bank. The investments Itaú made in disclosure and fair treatment of minority investors paid off handsomely: the company's stock price easily outperformed its peers, and it has been able to tap the Eurobond market to greatly reduce its overall cost of capital.

Commit to a Clear Governance Structure

In 2001, the family-run conglomerate Votorantim Group issued an annual report for the group as a whole. It established a new governance structure with a separate family council to deal with family-specific issues, leaving professional managers to run the businesses. Family transitions are delicate and can lead to internal problems that threaten the business. To avoid such problems, Votorantim is implementing a transition plan gradually and communicating the transition process broadly.

Make Transparency the Core of Your Organization

The Brazilian cosmetics company Natura made transparency the core of the entire organization as it transformed itself to compete in the 1990s. Facing the nationwide economic crisis in 1989 and the opening of the Brazilian economy a year later, Natura's three founders decided to anchor the company's transformation on the value of transparency. Management committed to a series of actions that were consistent with transparency. Seven branch offices were consolidated into one headquarters without walls, where everyone sat in cubicles and ate in the same cafeteria. The company focused its entire marketing campaign on transparency, under the motto "Truth in Cosmetics." For example, in marketing its Chronos line of antiwrinkle cream, the company used models who were older than thirty as well as real consumers. According to one cofounder: "We will not lie to you and tell you that you are going to look like Claudia Schiffer if you buy our products, but our ads tell you that you will still be beautiful."

The argument that "it pays to be transparent" is not an expression of naïve wishful thinking, but rather a cold, hard reality as global competition imposes transparency on companies. To compete globally, Chinese companies must increasingly yield to this pressure. When it comes to transparency, firms like Galanz represent the exception, creating an island of transparency in a sea of opacity. Chinese business as a whole has significant room to improve in terms of transparency. In a recent global survey conducted by the accounting firm PricewaterhouseCoopers, China scored second to last in terms of transparency, ahead of only Russia among the world's major economies.[14] Galanz was not the only transparent company in our sample, and the NASDAQ-listed companies (i.e., UTStarcom, AsiaInfo, and Sina) were forced to be transparent by investors and regulators as well. Other companies, such as Haier, were more of a mixed bag—internally transparent (recall the management rankings posted near the cafeteria door) but opaque in their reporting to financial markets.

How can companies become more transparent in a low-transparency country? Here managers in China (and elsewhere) have much to learn from best practices in Brazil, where a few outstanding companies have created islands of transparency in a sea of opacity (see box above).

Summary

This chapter discussed the costs and benefits of partnerships and argued that they shift constantly in volatile markets. It identified a series of concrete actions that entrepreneurs and executives can take to manage relationships dynamically. Key points are summarized in the following list.

- *Dynamic relationships* are the shifting balance of costs and benefits that characterize partnerships in unpredictable markets where interests among partners can shift dramatically and quickly. Benefits of such relationships include access to resources, reduction in investment, accelerated entry and exit, and risk sharing. However, relationships can also become shackles that limit a company's degrees of freedom.

- *Stretch relationships* are links with world-class partners that expose executives to best practices and force a company to approach this high level of performance itself. By actively seeking out and locking their organizations into stretch relationships, managers can pull their companies out of second-rate practices and help close the gap with global leaders in their industry.

- *Increased transparency* allows companies to attract and retain stretch partners. Executives in opaque markets such as China can make credible commitments to increase their firm's transparency, including opening their books, reporting more information than required, and instituting a clear governance structure.

SEVEN

Go for the Gold

RAPIDLY CHANGING MARKETS such as China periodically toss out golden opportunities to create and capture significant value in a short period. In a stable industry the duration between golden opportunities might be measured in decades. Consider the European tire industry. National champions such as Germany's Continental, Italy's Pirelli, and England's Dunlop came to dominate their respective home markets early in the twentieth century, and thereafter settled into relative stability through the 1960s. François Michelin, however, seized the golden opportunity created by a novel technology—the radial tire—to first dominate the French market, then consolidate the European market and subsequently emerge as a global leader.

Michelin's actions restructured an industry that had—despite two world wars and countless modest changes—remained remarkably stable for decades. In contrast to the tire industry, unpredictable markets such as China may produce golden opportunities once or twice a decade rather than once or twice a century. Given this relative frequency, Chinese entrepreneurs (and indeed managers in any unpredictable market) are likely to encounter at least one golden opportunity in their career. This chapter argues that seizing a golden opportunity can help a company survive and thrive in an unpredictable market, but requires a concentration of resources to pursue the opportunity. It uses the case of Chinese beverage leader Wahaha to illustrate these points.

Seizing the Future: The Wahaha Story

When Qinghou Zong took over a floundering factory in 1987, he never imagined that within a decade the Hangzhou Wahaha Group would emerge as one of China's leading beverage companies.[1] Wahaha carved out its leadership position in the face of fierce competition from both domestic upstarts and leading international beverage companies, including Coca-Cola, Nestlé, and PepsiCo. In 2003, Wahaha was China's market share leader in bottled water, fruit-flavored milk, and congee (a traditional thin gruel), competed in ready-to-drink tea and bottled fruit juices, and had established itself as a viable third player in the carbonated beverage market, after Coke and Pepsi. In 2003, the company reported revenues of $1.2 billion and pretax profits of $170 million, and produced 3.7 million tons of beverages, which ranked the company number five among beverage makers globally in terms of volume.

Qinghou Zong and the Birth of Wahaha

Wahaha's founder, Qinghou Zong, was born in 1945 and descended from a distinguished Chinese family. One ancestor, Tse Zong (1060–1128), was a prominent minister during the Song Dynasty (960–1279). His grandfather was the secretary of the treasury and governor of the Henan province in the administration of the warlord Zuoling Zhang (who controlled a portion of northeast China during the 1920s). Zong's father was an official with the Kuomintang government who could not find work after the Communists came to power. As a result, Zong's mother had to support the family of five children on a schoolteacher's modest salary.

After graduating from junior high school in 1963, Zong went to work on an isolated farm in Zhoushan, Zhejiang province. Zong decided to leave Hangzhou three years before the beginning of the Cultural Revolution to respond to the Party's call for educated youth to relocate to help China's farmers and, in part, to ease the financial burden on his mother. In his first year on the farm, Zong worked extracting and drying salt from a barren seashore, and then carrying the salt—balanced on a pole—for miles to the farm. After the farm went bankrupt in 1964, Zong was assigned to another farm in the same province, where he picked tea by hand, plowed the paddy fields, and baked bricks. Zong used his scarce leisure time to read books—mostly borrowed—including world and Chinese history and ancient and modern literature. During the Cultural Revolution, the only book available was the *Collected Work of Chairman Mao*, which Zong recalls reading hundreds of times.

In 1978, fifteen years after leaving his family, the thirty-three-year-old Zong was allowed to return to Hangzhou after the government instituted a policy allowing children in rural areas to take a position with their parents' employer as their elders retired from jobs in the city. After securing a residency permit, Zong joined the Hangzhou Affiliated Corrugated Fiber Box Factory, a collective enterprise associated with the elementary school where his mother had taught. Zong worked as a salesman and spent his days riding a tricycle-drawn cart from one school to the next, selling school supplies and ice cream bars for one fen (one-fifth of one cent) per bar. During his spare time, he studied management theory and completed his junior college education through a correspondence course.

In 1987, Zong's supervisor first promoted him to sales manager and then offered him the opportunity to take charge of a school-associated workshop that had not turned a profit in years. Zong later recalled his decision: "I was a 42-year-old man and worried that I was facing the last opportunity in my life. Although other people questioned my decision, I seized this precious opportunity like a hungry wolf." Zong hung up a wooden sign declaring the "School-Owned Factory in Shangcheng District of Hangzhou," borrowed a fund of $38,000 from the Shangcheng District Education Bureau, and hired two former teachers as his only employees, who worked out of cramped quarters in a school basement. The factory initially sold ice lollies, bottled water, and stationery to students at Shangcheng District. In 1987, Zong set up a small processing workshop to produce and sell nutritional drinks (based on a licensed recipe), which were very popular in China at that time.

Feeding China's "Little Emperors"

After establishing the factory, Zong quickly spotted what he saw as a golden opportunity. Through his frequent interaction with children, Zong realized that the government's one-child-per-family policy, in place since 1979, had the unexpected consequence of impairing children's nutrition. Coddled by their parents and grandparents, these so-called little emperors were extremely finicky—eating only foods that appealed to them, which were rarely the healthiest options. When Zong spoke to parents about the possibility of a nutritional drink aimed at improving children's appetite, he met with an enthusiastic response. Zong visited Professor Zhu at the Medical School of Zhejian University when he heard that the researcher had developed a formula for a nutritional drink tailored to children's needs. After numerous visits, Zong persuaded Zhu to share the formula and further develop it into a product. The product was positioned as a health supplement and was packaged in a glass vial, which was broken and the contents consumed like a medicine. Before launching the nutritional drink, Zong also commissioned a research institution to survey the health of over three thousand primary-school children—a survey that revealed nearly 45 percent of children were consuming less than the recommended levels of vitamins and minerals.

Although there were nearly three hundred nutritional drinks on the market already, none was targeted at children. To build awareness prior to the product launch, Zong announced a public competition in a local newspaper to come up with the best name for his new product. He ultimately selected "Wahaha" (which means "children laughing" in Chinese). Zong bet $54,000 (twice his available cash at the time) on an advertising campaign on the local television station with the simple slogan "Wahaha brings good appetite." Wahaha's advertisements also touted the findings of the children's nutrition survey showing that China's little emperors were not eating well despite family indulgence, and emphasized endorsements by prominent nutritional associations. After the first round of advertising, distributors literally gathered outside the factory gates clamoring for product. The factory's revenues exceeded $1 million in its first year selling the children's nutritional drink, and revenue increased more than fivefold the following year.

Wahaha's runaway market success quickly outstripped the factory's limited production capacity. In August 1991, municipal officials approached Zong about the possibility of acquiring the nearby Hangzhou Canned Food Factory, a state-owned enterprise that occupied a seventeen-acre production site and included food processing machinery. The officials were impressed with Wahaha's continued success and fed up with subsidizing the mounting losses suffered at the canning factory. Although relatively few state-owned enterprises had been privatized prior to 1991, Zong recognized the potential benefits to all parties, but also worried about the possible fallout with workers.

He was right to worry. Employees at state-owned enterprises had long enjoyed a set of rights that included lifetime employment, guaranteed benefits, and a healthy pension, collectively referred to as an "iron rice bowl." In the run-up to the acquisition, employees organized protests, plastered posters throughout Hangzhou inciting employees to protect their rights, and even formed armed "protection teams" in anticipation of resisting the acquisition by force if necessary. Zong worked closely with the local government and the workers and eventually won them over. Zong returned the plant to profitability within three months of the acquisition, receiving national media attention as one of the first examples of a "small fish eating a big one."

Expanding Products and Geographies

A few years after launching his offering, Zong grew concerned about the future of nutritional drinks. Although the product category still offered high margins and market growth, competitors were be-having irrationally, aggressively claiming benefits without sound sci-entific support and underwriting studies by research institutions to uncover problems with rivals' products. Price wars were depressing industry profits. Based on his assessment of the situation, Zong antic-ipated a crash in the nutritional drink market and began looking for a new product line. Zong decided to enter the children's soft drink market with a fruit-flavored milk, a combination of milk, juice pow-der, and vitamins. A local rival, Robust, had invested heavily to edu-cate the public about the health benefits of calcium-enriched milk, and Zong saw a "market behind the market" for milk that was both healthy and tasty.

At the end of 1991, Wahaha launched its first fruit milk, and soon after exited the children's nutritional supplement market to free resources to support the fruit milk introduction. Competitors were shocked that Wahaha would give up its leadership position, but Zong's assessment of the situation proved correct. The Ministry of Health investigated 212 nutritional supplements in 1995 and found that 70 percent provided no health benefits, while a significant number were actually dangerous. The results of the study, which were widely publi-cized in China, brought the entire sector into disrepute. Zong later explained this decision as an example of flexible adjustment of Wa-haha's strategy to the situation, a hallmark of the company's subse-quent moves.

To launch Wahaha Fruit Milk quickly, Zong initially focused on the Hangzhou market, where he pioneered free sample market-ing in China. Wahaha took out a large advertisement in the city's two largest-circulation papers announcing that consumers could ex-change the ad for a free bottle of fruit milk. A newspaper cost half as much as the milk, and readers quickly did the math. The newspapers had to print an additional 700,000 copies to meet demand, cus-tomers thronged the Wahaha headquarters, and Zong had to appear on local television to reaffirm Wahaha's intention to honor its pledge to all customers. Although the campaign resulted in initial losses, it created the product category of fruit-flavored milk and established Wahaha as the market leader.

To expand beyond the core market of Hangzhou, Zong began a nationwide campaign to introduce fruit milk. Zong framed his expansion as similar to a military campaign, in which he concentrated his attention and the company's resources on one city for a week and then moved on to the next city. Wahaha sales representatives would put a full-court press on the local government distributors, citing Wahaha's success in other markets, and if that failed, would contact every local distributor to create demand for the product. Zong would also focus his considerable marketing creativity on taking the city.

In one well-known example, Zong walked around the city of Zhengzhou looking for ways to build Wahaha's visibility. He noticed that the traffic was dangerous for children walking to school, and offered the local education authorities fifty thousand free yellow caps to increase students' visibility to drivers. Within a week, thousands of students around the city could be seen walking to school with yellow caps emblazoned with "donated by Wahaha." The "one week per city" campaign became famous, and Chinese business students pored over it as intently as their parents had studied Mao's military writings.

In 1994 the company's rapid growth in sales threatened Wahaha's future growth and even survival. Lacking the funds to build its own distribution network, Wahaha relied on local partners to distribute its products and was particularly strong in China's smaller cities, rural areas, and remote provinces. Providing credit to distributors, however, drained cash, and Wahaha sales representatives spent much of their time chasing delinquent accounts receivable rather than supporting distributors in the market. Zong initiated a novel program to manage accounts receivable, in which distributors were required to pay a deposit into an escrow account at the beginning of the year. Wahaha paid interest on the account (at rates above those offered by banks) and drew down the funds as products were delivered, in addition to offering customary discounts and rewards for early payment. This change in policy sifted out Wahaha's distributors, with cash-starved wholesalers dropping out of the network and stronger rivals self-selecting to stay with Wahaha.

Bolstered by the success in fruit milk, Zong decided to migrate the Wahaha brand from purely children's drinks to healthy beverages that adults would consume as well. In 1995, the company introduced enriched milk with vitamins A and D added, and promoted it for both children and health-conscious adults. Following quickly on the heels of that brand extension, Zong sensed that the bottled water market was poised to take off after multinationals had spent five years educating consumers on the benefits of distilled water and building their willingness to pay for a product with a free alternative.

To leverage its strength in rural distribution, Wahaha focused on single-serve bottled water rather than bulk water that was sold in jugs for use in urban homes and offices. Wahaha also undercut competitors' prices. To broaden the Wahaha brand's appeal beyond children to adults, the company shifted its advertising from memorable jingles to spots featuring popular musicians. To quickly seize the bottled water opportunity, Wahaha entered into an agreement with Danone and Peregrine Investment Holdings, which together provided $45 million in cash in five production joint ventures in exchange for a 51 percent stake in the ventures, cash dividends, and use of the Wahaha brand. (Danone subsequently acquired Peregrine's shares). Zong used the funds and access to Danone's technology to rapidly build production facilities nationwide to solidify its position in water before domestic competitors and multinationals could establish their position. Wahaha emerged as the market leader in bottled water and has maintained that position to the present.

An Exceptional Move: Introducing Future Cola

Wahaha's early successes in milk products and bottled water and later in juice and ready-to-drink tea all came outside the Chinese carbonated beverage market, which approximated the global market, where carbonates accounted for roughly one-half of total soft drink consumption. As in the rest of the world, Coca-Cola and PepsiCo dominated China's carbonated beverage market by the 1990s.[2] Coke established its first Chinese bottling operations in 1927, was forced out by the Communists in 1949, and was among the first American

consumer product companies to reenter China in 1979 when relationships between the two countries grew closer. Two years later
Pepsi entered the Chinese market, and together the two companies
rapidly vanquished local cola companies.

In the mid-1990s, however, Zong sensed that Chinese consumers
would support a local alternative to Coke and Pepsi. Taking a page
from Mao's book, Zong decided to focus on the rural areas, where
Wahaha enjoyed a relative advantage in distribution and brand recognition, while leaving the large cities to the multinationals. As usual,
Zong did his homework on the market, spending his typical two
hundred days per year in the field discussing the potential product
with distributors and customers, overseeing market research and thousands of taste tests, and cooperating with R&D institutes and leading
domestic flavor producers to create a product that was up to global
quality standards but was slightly sweeter and stronger in response
to local tastes.

Employees developed the name "Future Cola," whose Chinese
characters denote "exceptional." Others viewed Wahaha's move into
carbonated beverages as exceptional at best and suicidal at worst.
Robust, Wahaha's largest Chinese rival in bottled water, paid over a
million dollars to commission a study from a global management
consulting firm, which concluded that Coke and Pepsi could not be
beaten by a local upstart and advised Robust to avoid the carbonated
beverage market. Newspapers printed headlines that played on the
Future name, including "Exceptional Cola, Exceptional Disaster."

Zong was confident, however, and in June 1998, Wahaha launched
Future Cola with the tagline "the cola owned by the Chinese." Wahaha advertised on the national television channel CCTV 1, which
enjoyed a large audience and was particularly popular in rural areas.
The company also painted walls and hung posters in small villages to
promote the cola as an alternative to Coke and Pepsi. When the U.S.
military unintentionally bombed the Chinese Embassy in Belgrade in
May 1999, angry demonstrators protested throughout China, burned
American flags, and advocated boycotting U.S. products. Zong spotted an opportunity to promote his brand as the Chinese cola, and
shifted marketing funds to television advertisements to capitalize on

the mounting patriotism. The advertising paid off. Future Cola sales grew more than 30 percent in some key markets, and one consumer brought a small sum of money to his local TV station to voluntarily pay for Wahaha advertisements to show his support for Future Cola.

The success of the Future Cola launch surprised even Wahaha executives. The company experienced difficulties meeting demand, and outsourced production to outside bottlers. Wahaha built on its initial momentum by introducing other flavors of carbonated drinks under the Future brand. By 2003, the sales of Future carbonated beverages reached 620,000 tons, and Future emerged as the number three brand, with a 12 percent share in the carbonated drinks market according to the company's estimate. Wahaha, of course, faces challenges going forward, including dealing with more aggressive responses by Coke and Pepsi, maintaining momentum as Qinghou Zong delegates more responsibility to other managers, and expanding beyond the Chinese market. To date, however, the company has succeeded brilliantly in seizing a series of golden opportunities, including children's nutritional drinks, fruit milk, bottled water, and cola.

Go for the Gold

There is a saying among traders that sums up the logic of golden opportunities: "The small trades keep you in the game, but every once in a while a big opportunity comes along and that's where you make the real money." As you will recall from chapter 2, an opportunity is golden if it allows a firm to create significant value in a relatively short period of time. Golden opportunities differ from run-of-the-mill ones in their magnitude. Examples of golden opportunities among the companies in this book include major acquisitions (e.g., Haier's purchase of Red Star Enterprises), new technologies (e.g., UT-Starcom's Personal Access System, described in the next chapter), new product introductions (e.g., Legend's launch of Pentium-based computers), international expansion, and nationwide rollouts (e.g., Wahaha's Chinawide expansion in the mid-1990s).

Benefits of Seizing Golden Opportunities

It is possible that a firm can sustain the advantage from seizing an opportunity for an extended period, as Microsoft did when it established Windows as the dominant operating system for personal computers. In unpredictable markets such as China, however, the advantages resulting from seizing a golden opportunity are susceptible to sudden-death threats. The most common sudden-death threat in China occurs when a company seizes an opportunity, and its initial success induces dozens of competitors to enter the market. The new entrants precipitate a price war and eventually a shakeout in which many weaker players are weeded out. "In China, you need to anticipate that prices will fall, and build a business model that ensures sustainable profits and cash flow even after the price wars start," notes Simon Israel, the chairman of Danone's Asian-Pacific operations.[3] Advantages from seizing golden opportunities are also susceptible to disruptive technologies, major shifts in government policy, and a multinational's major thrust into China, among other factors. In short, gaining a sustainable competitive advantage by seizing a single golden opportunity is possible, but unlikely, and very difficult to predict in advance.[4]

Even when a golden opportunity fails to create a sustainable competitive advantage, it confers other important advantages in the here and now:

- *Providing windfall profits for investment.* Seizing a golden opportunity creates a spike in revenues that provides windfall profits a company can use to fortify its initial lead. After launching its children's nutritional beverage in 1988, for example, Wahaha increased its revenues from virtually nothing to nearly $19 million two years later. Zong recognized that his company's success would attract competitors who would spoil the party, and thus he prudently invested the profits in acquiring the assets of the canning factory and extending the Wahaha brand into fruit milk. Although Wahaha exited the children's nutrition segment, the windfall profits earned in a few years provided the foundation for future success.

- *Disorienting competitors.* When Wahaha launched its nutritional drink in October 1988, there were already at least three hundred companies in China selling nutritional drinks. None of them, however, targeted the children's market. By the time competitors reacted to Wahaha's market positioning, the company's brand already enjoyed nationwide recognition. In many cases, the speed with which a company seizes the initiative startles its competitors. When rival managers realize they are rapidly losing ground to their faster competitor in iterating through the SAPE cycle, they panic and either make foolhardy decisions or decide that defeat is inevitable and throw in the towel. Rapidly seizing a golden opportunity can fuel a self-fulfilling prophesy. A sudden gain by one firm causes rivals to panic, conclude their defeat is likely, and take actions that make their demise more likely. "The best battle," as Sun Tzu observed, "is the one that is never fought"—in this case, because your rival concludes you will win.

- *Attracting required resources.* Seizing a golden opportunity can also fuel a positive feedback cycle by attracting resources required for further success. Dramatic increases in revenue and market share create momentum, and potential partners, suppliers, or customers conclude the company is destined to lead the new market (or at a minimum survive the looming shakeout). This presumption of success attracts resources (e.g., money, partnerships, talent) to the company, and these resources increase the odds that it will, in fact, succeed. This creates a virtuous circle in which early success in exploiting a golden opportunity creates the presumption of ultimate victory, which attracts the resources making the victory more likely.

  As a practical matter, this virtuous circle means that potential customers, investors, and partners begin to knock on your door rather than you having to knock on theirs. This is precisely what happened with Wahaha. In the wake of its great success with product launch and turning around the Hangzhou canned food factory, Wahaha managers were approached by government officials in other provinces to take over failing factories in their regions. Similarly, Wahaha's early success attracted the attention of the Danone Group, which made significant investments in Wahaha beginning in 1996.

- *Positioning for subsequent opportunities.* People often think of opportunities as one-off events. Golden opportunities, however, emerge from a company's earlier actions and its ongoing reactions to a fluid situation. In Wahaha's case, school supplies led to nutritional drinks for children, which led to fruit milk, which led to bottled water, which led to cola. Success in seizing the earlier opportunities positioned Zong to spot subsequent opportunities and provided Wahaha with the resources (e.g., brand, distribution, production, expertise) to seize them.

Note that predictability is *not* among the benefits of seizing a golden opportunity. A company's future direction is difficult—perhaps impossible—to predict in advance. No entrepreneur peddling stationery and candy to schoolchildren in 1987 could have foreseen going head-to-head with Coke in just over a decade. Even the move from bottled water to cola was not foreordained: recall how Wahaha's rival Robust rejected that opportunity. It is a gross error to study a company's history of pursuing opportunities after the fact and assume that this progression was inevitable or even foreseeable beforehand. Imagine, for example, that Zong had decided to sell study guides to children rather than nutritional drinks. From where the company started in 1987, that opportunity would have seemed every bit as logical as nutritional drinks but would have set Wahaha onto a different path altogether. Business, to paraphrase the Danish philosopher Søren Kierkegaard, can only be understood backward, but it must be managed forward. Seizing a golden opportunity accelerates a company along a path but does not lift the fog of the future.

Golden Opportunities Require Concentration of Resources

Golden opportunities provide significant advantages, but there is a catch. Seizing a golden opportunity generally requires a concentration of the company's resources. *Concentration of resources* occurs when managers concentrate their available money, labor, and attention on a specific opportunity at a specific point in time to increase the odds of seizing the opportunity. Recall, for example, how Zong bet twice his available cash on advertisements to launch the Wahaha brand in Hangzhou. Zong's "one city per week" campaign is another small-scale example of concentrating his company's marketing staff, advertising spending, and his own attention to put a full-court press on one city's market before moving on to the next. Zong compares this approach to a commander of guerrilla forces summoning his widely dispersed forces from the hills to engage a traditional enemy in a classical battle at a set point in time.

The advantage of concentrating resources on a golden opportunity is obvious. By bringing all of a firm's resources to bear on a specific opportunity at a point in time, managers increase their impact and the odds that they will seize the opportunity. The disadvantages are equally clear. Concentration of resources leaves little in reserve and exposes a company to complete defeat. If Wahaha's nutritional drink had failed to gain traction in the market, the game would have been over before it had really begun. By declaring an opportunity "golden," moreover, a manager implies that it has a call on any or all of the resources required to succeed. Marshaling the resources necessary to succeed in the market often calls for difficult decisions. A firm may have to commit its entire war chest, as Zong did with the advertising, or exit from an established business to free resources for the golden opportunity—recall Wahaha's exit from children's nutritional drinks to support the fruit-milk launch. A company may have to give up ownership or control to quickly secure required resources from partners. Wahaha's success in bottled water, for example, was only possible because the company gave up a majority of equity in five joint ventures in exchange for the cash and technology required to strike quickly. In established companies, managers may need to kill projects or divert cash and talented managers from a profitable division to support the company's main effort.

Firms such as Microsoft or Wal-Mart may have large enough resource reserves to avoid these gut-wrenching choices. Most firms, however, lack such war chests, and as a result their managers must concentrate resources to seize golden opportunities. Moreover, they must make their big bets before it becomes perfectly clear whether the opportunity is as golden as they suspect. If they wait for complete certainty, rivals will seize the initiative. The bottom line is simple: seizing golden opportunities requires most executives to concentrate their resources despite imperfect information on the outcome. Make no mistake, these are gut-wrenching decisions. The entrepreneurs we interviewed repeatedly described concentrating resources to pursue golden opportunities as the most difficult and lonely decisions they ever made. Haier's Ruimin Zhang, for example, faced almost total resistance from other managers to his decision to acquire Red Star in 1995. In a few cases, these decisions took a physical toll and landed the entrepreneurs in the hospital.

Three Windows of Opportunity

Golden opportunities hold out the promise of great rewards but generally require the risky concentration of resources without the benefit of knowing whether the bet will pay off. The critical question is clear: How do entrepreneurs and managers recognize a golden opportunity from fool's gold before putting all their chips on the table to pursue it? The obvious questions are whether an unmet customer demand exists and how big the market might be if a company filled that demand. Zong, for example, knew from personal experience that parents were concerned about their little emperors' nutrition, and calculated that he could make a killing even if he served only a modest fraction of the country's 300 million children.

These questions of whether the customer need is real and the potential market big enough to constitute a golden opportunity are critical. They are also painfully obvious, and we add little by reminding managers to address them. The tougher question is whether the timing is right to concentrate resources to pursue the opportunity. People often use the phrase *window of opportunity* to describe a time period during which an opportunity must be seized or lost (perhaps forever). The notion of a window that opens for a while and then closes highlights the fleeting nature of opportunities, where timing is everything. Too early can be as bad as too late.

The reality of golden opportunities, however, is more complicated. Entrepreneurs and managers must consider not just one, but multiple, windows of opportunity—including customers, competitors, capital markets, technical evolution, and government policy among others. To further complicate matters, these windows vary in importance over time and are constantly shifting—opening a crack or threatening to close altogether. As a result, entrepreneurs must get the timing right to get through the windows that matter.

To simplify the task of evaluating the timing, it is helpful to focus on three windows of opportunity, specifically customers, competitors, and context (including external factors other than buyers and rivals), which consistently matter in evaluating whether the timing is right to pursue an opportunity. Many people have discussed time-based competition, in which the faster rival beats the slower. The three windows of opportunity model, in contrast, focuses on *timing-based competition*. There is no assumption that faster always trumps slower. Wahaha, for example, pioneered the children's nutritional drink segment. In other cases, however, Wahaha followed early entrants who educated consumers on the benefits of enriched milk, bottled waters, and cola. Success depends on concentrating resources on the right opportunity at the right time. Getting the timing right, to a large extent, requires managers to make their move when all three factors are aligned. Timing will, of course, also be influenced by internal factors (which are the focus of the next chapter). Much of timing, however, depends on forces largely outside the control of an entrepreneur or manager.

Although there is no one-size-fits-all list of questions to assess whether the timing is right for all opportunities, the following questions can help managers to think about the factors that influence whether it is the right time to make a move.

- *Is the market poised to take off?* Timing the introduction of a new good or service is not an exact science, but there are steps managers and entrepreneurs can take to increase the odds that they get it right. Trial customers can provide insights into whether the market might be ready: if one customer wants a new good or service, the odds are that others will as well. To avoid jumping in too early, executives can wait for first movers to validate the market. To avoid being too late, they can rapidly and aggressively enter before another competitor establishes a leadership position.[5] Wahaha was not the first entrant in the bottled water market—Zong let others test the waters and educate consumers. When he was convinced that the market was poised to take off, however, Zong aggressively secured resources from Danone to support Wahaha's bottled water offering.

    To differentiate Wahaha's offering from early leaders when entering a market, Zong looks for what he calls "the market behind the market." When entering the nutritional drink market, for example, Zong explicitly rejected the option of following the existing competitors by being the 301st competitor to offer a general nutritional drink. Instead, he was the first to offer a product targeted to children. Similarly, when Wahaha launched its first adult milk product in 1995, Robust had already invested in educating consumers about the benefits of calcium. As a latecomer to the general milk market, Wahaha launched "AD Milk" enriched with calcium and nutrients to enhance absorption as well.

- *What is the phrase that pays?* The discipline of describing the opportunity in a short (five words or fewer) phrase forces the entrepreneur or manager to strip away the peripheral aspects and distill an opportunity to its essence. The phrase that pays can help assess whether the timing is right. If potential customers instantly understand your formula and find it fresh and exciting, you may have hit the sweet spot of timing. If they understand the formula but say it is obvious, stale, or clichéd, then you are probably one step behind the market. If they think it sounds great in theory but doesn't resonate with them at a gut level, then you may be two or more steps ahead of the market. This process can also help you screen potential customers or investors who "get it" and would be good partners to work with in pursuing the opportunity.

- *Is there already an entrenched competitor?* One of the most fundamental insights of military theory is the danger of engaging in conflict with strong and deeply entrenched enemies. Sun Tzu captured this with his famous maxim that military tactics are like flowing water; because water in its natural course flows on when it hits resistance and rushes in when it encounters a gap.[6] Mao followed this approach when the Communists initially avoided the cities, where the Nationalists were strong, and swarmed the rural areas, where they were weak. Zong followed the identical approach when he launched carbonated beverages. Wahaha avoided the cities, where Coke and Pepsi were strong, while concentrating resources on the rural areas, where they were relatively weaker. It is, of course, impossible to find segments where there are no rivals at all. Golden opportunities will always attract many entrants. The key is to avoid terrain where a strong competitor has already staked out a position and fortified it with resources such as brand or distribution.

- *How quickly will competitors spot the opportunity?* The question is not whether strong competitors will notice a golden opportunity—they always do if its truly golden—but *when* they'll spot it. Sometimes competitors' strategic frames slow their opportunity recognition. Strategic frames are mental models dictating how executives interpret their industry, competitors, customers, and strengths. Existing frames influence how quickly executives identify new opportunities. In assessing the speed of potential rivals' response, you should try to understand their strategic frames—how they are likely to interpret the situation, and when they will spot the opportunity. This gives you some estimate of how much time you have. Good competitors may fail to notice golden opportunities for various reasons. They might simply lack the situational awareness necessary to spot an opportunity. Expatriate managers, for example, would have had little chance of understanding how China's one-child policy would lead to malnutrition. Foreign competitors may view the Chinese market through the lens of their home market, making them slow to spot local opportunities. At some point, of course, competitors will wake up, smell the opportunity, and bring their resources to bear.

Part of getting the timing right is staying under rivals' radar screen long enough to dig in before they respond. At that point, it may be too costly for even deep-pocket competitors to dislodge an early entrant. Companies can buy time by framing the opportunity as outside their rivals' core business.[7] Internet pioneer Netscape, for instance, rushed to an early lead by framing its software as a "Web browser" compatible with Microsoft's operating system. When Netscape's CEO reframed the company's product as a "desktop" alternative to Microsoft's products, he put his start-up squarely in the cross-hairs of the richest and most feared software company in history with predictable results.

- *Do competitors have incentives to pursue an opportunity right now?* Rivals may lack the incentives to pursue an opportunity even if they notice it. The market size may be too small relative to alternatives. The multinational personal computer companies, for example, all knew China was an important potential market in the 1980s, but the market was still small relative to Japan, North America, and Western Europe, which were booming with explosive growth. Pursuing a golden opportunity may also force established players to destroy their current profit base. Zong, for example, reckoned that Coke would sacrifice market share in rural areas rather than sacrifice profits by matching Future Cola's lower prices. The new opportunity may not serve the needs of a competitor's existing customers, and therefore may fail to gain funding.[8]

- *Can competitors pounce right now?* Sometimes good companies see an opportunity, have strong incentives to pursue it, and still fail to execute. Rivals may, of course, simply lack the resources required to pursue an opportunity. Recall how computer maker Great Wall was so battered by the onslaught of multinationals in the early and mid-1990s that it could not match Legend's decisive moves to gain market share. Internal management turmoil can also temporarily hobble a worthy rival. Galanz made its move in microwaves while Whirlpool was integrating acquisitions and temporarily unable to respond quickly. The key phrase in this question is "right now." Competitive gaps, like unmet customer demand, are fleeting. Management turmoil at a competitor might last a year, but it won't last forever. The best time to strike may be right after a competitor has committed to an alternative opportunity. Again, this won't prevent them from going after your golden opportunity forever, but it might slow them down long enough for you to establish a lead and dig in.

- *How will you defend your position?* Suppose you can beat your competitors to the punch and establish an early lead; how will you defend that beachhead against the inevitable attack by competitors? Can you develop a strong distribution network, process expertise, brand recognition, proprietary technology, deep relationships with customers, or other resources that will keep rivals at bay? In a dynamic market such as China, it will be impossible to sustain these defenses forever. It is, however, critical to consider how you can fortify your position long enough to build a war chest to seize the next golden opportunity or survive sudden-death threats.

- *Why is the $20 bill still on the ground?* An old joke describes two economists walking down the street. The first one looks down and exclaims, "There is a $20 bill on the ground." The other one turns to him and says, "That's impossible. If it were there, someone would have picked it up already." The joke reveals an important insight from economics—if opportunities are attractive, someone will seize them rapidly. The joke also raises an important question: if this really *is* a golden opportunity, why hasn't someone seized it already? Of course, someone has to be first. But given the number of entrepreneurs in the world, the odds are low that it is you. Odds are that the timing is either too late or too early.

  There are, however, convincing answers to the question. The most compelling answer to the question of why the $20 bill is on the ground is that a change in the broader context is just now creating the opportunity. The need for children's nutritional drinks, for example, arose from China's one-child policy. Demand for bottled water arose, in part, from the degradation of drinking water resulting from rapid industrialization. Growing nationalist sentiment created demand for a Chinese cola, which spiked with the bombing of the Chinese embassy in Belgrade. Before concentrating their resources, entrepreneurs and managers should ask themselves what changed in the regulatory, market, technical, or social context to generate this opportunity right now. If they cannot point to a specific change, the apparent golden opportunity may be fool's gold.

Summary

This chapter argued that companies can gain significant advantages from seizing golden opportunities but must generally concentrate their resources to do so. The three windows of opportunity framework can help managers and entrepreneurs evaluate opportunities to increase the odds of getting their timing right when pursuing a golden opportunity. Key points from this chapter are summarized in the following list. The next chapter discusses how companies can scale rapidly when the moment is right. We illustrate the notion of getting big right with the story of UTStarcom.

- The *benefits of seizing a golden opportunity* include windfall profits for further investment and the possibility of disorienting competitors, attracting resources required for future competition, and positioning a company to seize subsequent opportunities. Golden opportunities may confer a sustainable competitive advantage, but that is unlikely and will only be established after the fact.

- *Future direction remains unpredictable* even after a company has seized a golden opportunity. It is a gross error to study a company's history of pursuing opportunities after the fact and assume that this progression was inevitable and obvious beforehand. Seizing a golden opportunity does set a company on a path, but the trajectory of that path is not obvious in advance.

- *Concentration of resources* occurs when managers concentrate their available money, labor, and attention on a specific opportunity at a specific point in time to increase the odds of seizing the opportunity. Marshaling required resources demands difficult decisions, and concentration of resources exposes a company to the possibility of complete defeat.

- The *three windows of opportunity* is a framework that focuses on questions about customers, competitors, and context that help managers evaluate whether the timing is right to bet big on pursuing a golden opportunity.

EIGHT

Get Big Right

T HIS CHAPTER discusses how to get big right, that is, how to scale a business effectively when pursuing a golden opportunity. Before beginning, it is worth pausing to summarize why getting big right is so important in unpredictable markets. Companies advancing through the fog of the future, you will recall, encounter a steady stream of opportunities of varying magnitude, including the periodic golden opportunity. Conducting reconnaissance into the future allows entrepreneurs and managers to identify gaps in the market before rivals. When they come across a potentially vast gap in the market, they can consider the three windows of opportunity—customers, competitors, and the broader context—to gauge the potential to create value and assess whether the time is right to concentrate resources.

Even after they identify a gap in the market, decide that the external factors are propitious, and concentrate their resources, entrepreneurs often stumble because they cannot scale their organization to meet booming customer demand before competitors rush into the market and dislodge them. To use a military metaphor, a general must not only spot a gap in the enemy's defense and mass troops in time and space to win a battle, but also must reinforce the initial position to hold the ground. The rapid growth required to seize a golden opportunity before rivals places enormous strains on a company's resources. Entrepreneurs may face big-company problems for the first time, for example, or struggle to raise the money required to fund growth. Successfully seizing a golden opportunity requires companies to overcome the myriad challenges inherent in rapid growth. This chapter discusses how entrepreneurs and managers can think more systematically about the challenges of scaling their organization, illustrating these insights with the example of UTStarcom.

The UTStarcom Story

UTStarcom was founded in 1995 through the merger of two telecommunications start-ups headquartered in the United States but focused on the Chinese market.[1] The company's revenues grew from $10 million in 1995 to $2 billion in 2003, which landed UTStarcom a place on the 2003 *Fortune* 1000 (see figure 8-1 for historical revenues). UTStarcom achieved its rapid growth by developing and selling its "Personal Access System," which enables cordless phones to rove up to sixty miles within a city limit. Of course, major telecommunications players such as Ericsson, Motorola, Nokia, and Alcatel provide mobile telephone backbones and handsets. UTStarcom's solution, however, works on a fixed-line infrastructure, which allows telephone service providers such as China Telecom to offer end users high-quality wireless service without heavy investment in capital goods. At the end of 2003, UTStarcom's equipment served over 20 million customers in China and accounted for approximately 70 percent of the country's fixed-line wireless business.

The Foundation of UTStarcom

UTStarcom traces its roots back not to one entrepreneur, but to two—Hong Lu and Ying Wu, who independently founded the two companies that would later merge to become UTStarcom. Hongliang

FIGURE 8-1

UTStarcom revenues ($ millions)

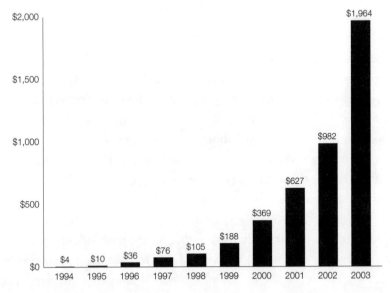

Source: Company documents.

(Hong) Lu came to China via a roundabout route. Born in Taiwan and educated in Japan, Lu came to the United States at the age of eighteen to study, although he could not speak the language and had not been accepted by a college. To improve his English, Lu enrolled in Berkeley High School, where his classmates scoffed at his ambition to attend the highly selective University of California, Berkeley. Lu persisted, however, supporting himself as a dishwasher and night manager at an Oakland ice cream store, and was accepted by Berkeley to study civil engineering.

When he graduated from college, Lu chose to work for Masayoshi Son, who would go on to found Softbank and enjoy a few days as the wealthiest man in the world at the height of the Internet bubble. Today, of course, graduates dream of the chance to work with Son. In 1978, however, this was a risky career move at best. Son, still an economics student at Berkeley, made his first million importing arcade games from Japan and installing them around Berkeley's campus. Lu served as a project manager for a new venture, which required him to work with a Berkeley physics professor and his doctoral students who were hired by Son to develop a multilingual pocket-size translator (which eventually became the prototype for Sharp's Wizard). As if supervising doctoral students on a challenging software project wasn't a daunting enough task for a recently minted civil engineer, Lu grew increasingly nervous when his first two checks from Son bounced. Again Lu persevered, took over the venture's bookkeeping, and eventually bought Son's share of the resulting company—Unison—when Son returned to Japan in 1981 to found Softbank. Lu spent the following decade running Unison, including a stint as the head of a joint venture with Japan's Kyocera International.

Lu sold his stake to Kyocera in 1990 and decided to take a year to look for an opportunity for another start-up outside the personal computer industry, which he avoided due to chronically low profits. In 1991, Lu visited the People's Republic of China for the first time. When he tried to place a call from Beijing to Shenzhen, he found that he had to dial a hundred times to get a line. Where others saw only an annoyance, Lu spotted a golden opportunity. Later that year, Lu founded Unitech Industries in Alameda, California, to produce telecommunications equipment for the Chinese market, raised angel funding, recruited Chinese engineers from Bell Labs to staff the company, and built a small production facility in Hangzhou.

That same year, Ying Wu founded a start-up to pursue the same opportunity. Ying Wu was born in Beijing to a teacher's family. After receiving his bachelor's degree in electrical engineering from Beijing University of Technology, Wu took a teaching job at his alma mater. Three years later in 1985, he left China to pursue a master's degree at the New Jersey Institute of Technology. Wu left China with $30 in his pocket, the cap at that time on currency students could take out of the country, and landed in New Jersey $3 poorer, after spending $1 for a beer on the plane and donating $2 to a charity worker at the airport, who mistook Wu for a Japanese businessman and insisted on a donation. After completing his master's degree in electrical engineering, Wu worked with AT&T Bell Labs (now part of Lucent Technologies) and Bellcore (now Telcordia) for five years.

In 1991, Wu spotted the opportunity to provide telecommunications equipment to China and founded Starcom Network Systems with another Chinese engineer from Bell Labs. Wu later recalled their analysis: "The teledensity [telephones per capita] in China at that time was 1.7 percent, and that in the United States was 76 percent. We figured if China reached 50 percent teledensity, there would be six hundred million users—three times bigger than the U.S. market at that time." In late 1991, Wu set up Starcom, returned to China to start securing orders, and established a research and development center in Iselin, New Jersey, to design access equipment and telecom software.

Unitech Telecom and Starcom independently achieved revenues of a few million dollars in their first few years of operation. In 1995, Wu had dinner with Bill Huang, a former employee at Bell Labs then working with Unitech. Huang told his former boss that the two companies complemented each other well and were ideal partners for a merger. Starcom focused on software, enjoyed strong relationships at the ministry and provincial levels, and had strong marketing skills. Unitech, in contrast, developed hardware, had good relationships at the regional and county levels, and brought strong financial and management skills. After brief discussions, Lu and Wu agreed to combine the two companies into UTStarcom, with corporate headquarters in Alameda, research facilities in New Jersey and Shenzhen, production in Hangzhou, and finance, marketing, and sales operations in Beijing. Lu took the position of president and CEO, while Wu became vice chairman of the board and executive vice president in charge of the company's Chinese subsidiary when UTStarcom was formed in October 1995. Prior to the merger, the founders made a thirty-minute presentation to Masayoshi Son, who decided to invest $30 million for a 30 percent stake in the new company, a funding round referred to by Wu and Lu as "30-30-30."

UTStarcom Takes Off with "Little Smart"

Although UTStarcom was incorporated in the United States and conducted research there, it was focused on serving the hundreds of millions of potential customers that would emerge as China's telephone penetration moved toward the level found in Western countries. Initially, UTStarcom sold a variety of different products in China, which provided them with a foothold in the market but did not generate significant sales. In 1995 and 1996, Wu and Lu spent most of their time in China speaking with local telecommunication providers and end customers, looking for their opening. Based on their research, Lu and Wu estimated that China's wealthiest 20 percent would purchase full-service mobile telephones, whereas the poorest 30 percent could not afford any service whatsoever. This left 50 percent of China's consumers as a potential market if they could develop a system to serve them at the right price. They also noticed that a large percentage of China's urban population worked and lived in a tight area (perhaps a dozen square kilometers) and rarely traveled very far or very fast, relying primarily on bikes and taxis for transport.

Wu and Lu initially planned to develop and produce equipment that would provide limited mobility at low cost based on a technology known as wireless local loop (WLL) that allowed subscribers to access the fixed-line telephone network remotely with handsets resembling mobile phones. Picture a cordless phone with a range of a few kilometers from its cradle. Wireless local loop had won only limited acceptance in Western markets, in part because it could not maintain service when subscribers traveled at high speeds on highways. This technical limitation represented a relatively minor annoyance for many Chinese consumers who spent most of their time within a small perimeter and traveled short distances by foot, bicycle and cars (which were often slowed by city traffic). UTStarcom executives envisioned creating interconnected networks of users in small neighborhoods who could carry their home phones while visiting local shops. Alternately, office workers could carry their work phones anywhere within a building. They dubbed their system the "wireless community phone."

Lu and Wu were, however, disappointed by customers' response. Preliminary discussions with China Telecom executives and end users revealed that they viewed the wireless community phone as little more than a long-range cordless phone—a product that generated limited enthusiasm. Through their discussions, however, the UTStarcom team spotted a much larger opportunity. What if they could develop a system that linked local loops, thereby extending the range of mobility beyond a neighborhood or building to encompass an entire city? UTStarcom's research team evaluated existing WLL technologies to determine whether any could be interconnected to extend their range. They quickly focused on the Personal Handy Phone System (known in the acronym-obsessed telecommunications industry as PHS). Developed in Japan, this technology enjoyed a brief spurt of success in the mid-1990s before being replaced by cellular telephones. Working in New Jersey, UTStarcom's research team was able to modify the existing technology to create a working prototype within three months.

The new system, dubbed the Personal Access System (PAS), held several attractions for China Telecom, the country's dominant telecommunications service provider. The capital expenditure required to install a PAS system was much lower than the investment required to offer full mobility, because UTStarcom's solution used existing switches and billing systems. Moreover, many people (including Wu and Lu) expected China Telecom to be stripped of its existing mobile telephone operations by regulators intent on stimulating competition. Two new carriers—China United Telecommunications (China Unicom) and Jitong Communications—had been created in 1994 to offer services, including cellular, to break the existing monopoly. If China Telecom did lose its mobile business (which indeed occurred in 1997), PAS could help the remaining fixed-line business retain existing customers and attract new ones by offering limited mobility on its existing infrastructure. The PAS's technical specifications also allowed rapid deployment and could scale from one hundred users to over 2 million.

Despite PAS's potential benefits, Lu and Wu struggled to convince customers to take a chance on an unproven technology from a start-up whose revenues represented rounding error for global players such as Lucent, Nortel, or Alcatel. Fortunately, Wu and Lu had thousands of potential customers to woo. China Telecom was a state-owned enterprise regulated by the Ministry of Information Industry, which oversaw approximately 2,400 local telecommunications bureaus that provided their communities with voice (and in some cases data) access services. These local operators enjoyed great autonomy in purchasing, installation, and operating decisions. UTStarcom's founders worked this decentralized purchasing process and ultimately convinced the local operator in Yuhang to pilot the system. Yuhang and small-scale installations in other cities allowed UTStarcom to refine the technology, its business model, and marketing. After iterating through several names to market its handset to consumers, for example, UTStarcom ultimately settled on Xiao Ling Tong, or "Little Smart Phone."

The early installations of PAS service in 1997 exceeded UTStarcom's most optimistic forecasts. Subscribers were delighted that they paid no connection fee, made outgoing calls at fixed-line rates, and avoided the charge for incoming calls levied by China Mobile and China Unicom. Taken together, these savings allowed subscribers to enjoy the limited mobility of PAS at approximately one-fifth the cost of cellular service. The PAS phones offered benefits in addition to lower price, including longer battery life (typically two weeks in standby mode) and lower radiation.

The rapid market acceptance of early PAS installations encouraged other provincial operators to evaluate the service for large towns and small cities. Additional pressure to consider PAS came in 1997 when China Telecom's cellular business was spun off into an independent entity named China Mobile, with cellular telephone assets in the Guangdong and Zhejiang provinces, and raised $4.2 billion from an initial public offering on the Hong Kong and New York stock exchanges. Local fixed-line operators looked for ways to compete with their newly created, deep-pocket rival, and UTStarcom's technology provided one possible solution. The company's big break came in 1999, when UTStarcom received an order from the operator in Xian to serve four hundred thousand subscribers, a step-function increase over previous orders that had ranged from a few thousand to ten thousand subscribers.

As the sole provider of PAS equipment to China Telecom at the time, UTStarcom reaped all the benefits of increased demand, and the company's revenues surpassed $100 million in 1998, increasing to $369 million by 2000. Wu and Lu recruited several seasoned executives to help manage the growth, including Johnny Chou, a Princeton-educated manager at Bell Labs, who joined UTStarcom as vice president of engineering and quickly rose to the COO position for the Chinese operations. The company built a nationwide network of sales and technical support offices to keep up with booming demand and funded its growth through several rounds of fundraising, including $160 million from Softbank in 1998, $60 million from Intel in 1999, and $207 million in an initial public offering on NASDAQ in March 2000.

The commercial success of PAS complicated life for China Telecom, which had never been granted a mobile service license. China Telecom marketed PAS as a supplement to fixed-line phones rather than a full-fledged wireless service. To avoid any run-ins with regulators who might interpret things differently, China Telecom initially abstained from rolling out PAS in major cities such as Shanghai, Beijing, and Guangzhou. The mobile carriers China Mobile and China Unicom, however, still felt the heat and lobbied the Ministry of Information Industry. They argued that PAS represented a de facto mobile service that required the mobile license that China Telecom lacked. No license, they argued, no PAS.

Their lobbying paid off. On May 31, 2000, the ministry announced an investigation into PAS service and required all local China Telecom operators to halt new PAS deployment pending the results of the inquiry. UTStarcom's stock plummeted 46 percent in the next day of trading. One month later, the Ministry of Information Industry declared that it had officially defined PAS as a "small coverage, low speed, mobile wireless access service" that could, however, be deployed in certain regions but not in large cities. UTStarcom's market value recovered approximately half of its lost value, while China Mobile and China Unicom plunged on that day. On November 21, 2000, the Ministry of Information Industry issued another announcement requiring China Telecom to raise tariffs for PAS service—a ruling that local operators largely ignored.

Diversifying Products and Markets

UTStarcom continued to ride the growth of PAS. The Ministry of Information Industry split China Telecom's assets to create a second land-line provider, China Netcom, and competition between them spurred further demand for PAS systems. In late 2003, the Ministry of Information Industry allowed both land-line telecoms to launch PAS service in major cities such as Beijing, Shanghai, and Guangzhou, thereby opening up a market of 45 million residents that had been officially off-limits for PAS up to then. Nationwide, PAS subscriptions grew from 1.6 million subscribers in 2000 to 45 million in September 2004.

The booming PAS market attracted competition, including multinational Lucent and local rival ZTE. Despite the increased competition, UTStarcom executives believed their equipment accounted for approximately 60 percent of new systems sold. Industry analysts, however, predicted that UTStarcom could not rely on PAS sales in China to maintain historical levels of revenue growth. China Telecom and China Netcom—UTStarcom's largest customers—were planning to shift future investment to building third-generation cellular networks after receiving licenses, and end users at the high end of the market were expected to select third-generation cellular networks over PAS systems as the new technology became available.

Lu and Wu recognized that UTStarcom's initial growth had been driven by a single technology sold in a single market. They looked for new opportunities to diversify their revenues and maintain future growth by extending both their geographic and product mix. UTStarcom executives followed a set of simple rules in selecting which opportunities to pursue. First, they would sell new products to established customers and established products to new customers, but avoid selling new products to new customers. Thus, selling non-PAS switches to China Telecom and selling PAS systems in India were both acceptable options, but selling new switches in India was not an option. Second, products had to become number one or two in their market within three years, or the company would kill them. Third, the company would only pursue opportunities that it could scale quickly, measured concretely by achieving $50 million in revenues within the first three years. Fourth, UTStarcom would only offer products based on the Internet Protocol (IP), since the company's executives believed that all applications, including voice, data, and media, would eventually converge on a single network using the Internet Protocol. Fifth, all new products had to offer unique features rather than offering me-too equipment and competing on price.

UTStarcom followed these rules to develop new products that included equipment to allow land-line telecommunication companies such as China Telecom to provide broadband Internet, voice, and television over wire lines using the Internet Protocol (also known as IP-DSLAM, or IP-based digital subscriber line access multiplexer, for acronym aficionados). UTStarcom supplemented its internal research by acquiring companies for their technology, including the 2003 purchase of the CommWorks division from networking pioneer 3Com. In 2003, the Ministry of Information Industry selected UTStarcom as one of twelve companies qualified to develop third-generation networks in China.

UTStarcom also sought to grow through international expansion. It made its first international sale in 2000 when it sold a $35 million PAS system to a Taiwanese service provider. Company executives set an aggressive target of increasing international sales from 15 percent of total revenues in 2003 to 50 percent by 2007, and sold PAS equipment in emerging markets such as Vietnam, Thailand, Brazil, and Mexico. India was a particular focus for the company. Like China, India was a developing country with over a billion inhabitants. India's telecommunications market lagged behind China's, with 4.4 percent fixed-line telephones per capita versus 21 percent for China and 76 percent for the United States. Penetrating the Indian market posed challenges, however, including obstacles to regulatory approval and technical challenges in serving a population that was less geographically concentrated than China's. In 2004, UTStarcom had two R&D centers in India, employing over two hundred engineers.

Get Big Right

UTStarcom, like any company competing in China's dynamic tele-communications equipment industry, faces challenges going forward. It is not clear that telecom service providers will trust the company for third-generation solutions, that PAS will work as well in other emerging markets as it has in China, or that management will be able to execute as effectively on future opportunities as it has on PAS. UTStarcom's success to date has largely resulted from a tight focus on seizing the golden opportunity offered by PAS, and management runs the risk of losing its way as it attempts to simultaneously introduce new products and conquer new markets.

Regardless of how the story plays out going forward, UTStarcom has succeeded admirably in scaling its business from $10 million to $2 billion in eight years, exceeding equity analysts' consensus revenue and profit forecasts for seventeen consecutive quarters after going public. This performance is particularly impressive when one recalls the crises encountered by such respected firms as Dell Computers and Oracle as they attempted to scale their operations during similar periods of revenue growth. UTStarcom's impressive performance in growing revenues rapidly without a hiccup illustrates some broader lessons about how companies can effectively scale their operations.

Have a Clear Focus

Clarity of focus and the discipline to stick with it were critical to UTStarcom's ability to get big right. Putting all your eggs in one basket runs counter to the notion of diversification as a tool to manage risk in unpredictable markets. Investors diversify their portfolio of stocks to manage risk, and venture capitalists spread their investments across several companies, betting on a few winners to compensate for several losers. Although it is a prudent approach for investors, diversification is dangerous when a company decides to pursue a golden opportunity. Concentration of resources in time and in a market is required to fill a gap before competitors do so. UT-Starcom's few hundred employees were laughably few compared with the staffing levels of established telecommunication equipment providers such as Lucent, Alcatel, and Nortel in the late 1990s. The start-up, however, was completely focused on understanding and serving the market for low-price, mobile products employing land lines. Attempting to be all things to all customers, in contrast, would have spread the company's limited resources too thin.

Clarity of focus not only enables concentration of current re-sources but also makes it easier to grow the organization by provid-ing guidance on what not to do. Many entrepreneurs and managers begin with the assumption that they must do everything themselves, and then think about what activities they might outsource. UTStar-com's founders turned this logic on its head and focused exclusively on those activities that allowed them to satisfy the unmet need for fixed-line mobile services at an affordable price. They relied on part-ners for everything else. Rather than attempting to develop the tech-nology themselves, for example, they scoured the globe for existing wireless local loop technology that could be modified to serve the needs of China's consumers. Once they settled on a technology, they further focused their efforts on developing only the equipment that served as the interface between existing land-line switches and base stations. UTStarcom initially sourced the PAS base stations and hand-sets from Sanyo and Mitsubishi and resold them as part of an inte-grated system to the local telephone operators. UTStarcom's narrow focus simplified the challenge of scaling because the company only had to ramp up development and manufacturing of the interface equipment. Much larger companies were responsible for increasing production of the base stations and handsets.

Very few companies find their focus right off the bat. Most entre-preneurs iterate through several business models before they find the one that solves customer needs, provides a leg up on competitors, and makes financial sense.[2] UTStarcom was no exception. Both Lu and Wu began exploring China's telecommunications market in 1991 and spent a few years offering a variety of products while look-ing for a gap in the market. Even after recognizing the opportunity to adapt wireless local loop technology to provide low-cost mobile service on existing infrastructure, they still needed to refine their business model from the "community phone" to the Little Smart Phone that covered an entire city. Few start-ups bypass this period of experimentation. Indeed, a common mistake among both start-ups and established companies is to overcommit resources before the business model has stabilized. In fact, entrepreneurs, managers, and investors should be very nervous about any attempt to scale a business model that has not gone through at least one major (and several minor) revisions. Scaling a business model before it is stabilized will definitely surface its problems, but will leave little time to solve them. It is much better to iterate through experiments and refine and stabilize the model before attempting to get big.

Standardize What Matters

In the early years of a venture, entrepreneurs spend much of their lives fighting fires and scrambling to survive. They rarely enjoy the luxury of time to consider how to systematize the processes within their organization, and their time would probably be better spent on pressing issues anyway. As they move beyond the initial period of experimentation, however, entrepreneurs often find that the ad hoc processes that worked fine in the start-up phase break down under the strain of rapid growth when scaling. Obvious examples are customer service and production. UTStarcom's top executives, for example, personally fielded customer complaints and helped assemble equipment for the first few installations of PAS systems. This level of personal involvement was, of course, unsustainable as UTStarcom's customer list escalated into the hundreds. At this point, Lu and Wu needed to put in standardized systems that could consistently and reliably perform routine operations without top executive attention. Predictable execution not only frees top executives' time but also confers efficiency and the legitimacy that results from consistent execution. Standardization can also facilitate coordination across different departments within a growing organization and with customers and suppliers.

This is not, of course, an argument for standardizing everything. Writing down a step-by-step standard operating procedure for sending overnight mail is clearly over the top. Standardization should be limited to key activities that attract and retain customers, keep costs down, or differentiate the company from competitors. A useful discipline when standardizing is to think like a big company as you're beginning to scale. Even when UTStarcom was a small company, for example, top executives routinely asked whether proposed processes would still work when the company had a few hundred installations. It is also important to note that standardization applies to more than just production processes and logistics. In fact, scaling generally requires a company to standardize across five distinct elements of the organization.[3]

1. *Processes* are the repeated procedures that companies use to get work done, including formal routines, such as manufacturing or logistics, and less formal processes, such as resource allocation and decision making.[4] Standardizing processes increases efficiency, enables replication, and facilitates coordination among different parts of an organization. In February 2004, for example, UTStarcom launched a process to standardize procurement procedures, including a reverse auction in which vendors bid for business, followed by a formal review of all listed vendors to ensure quality and performance. The standardized procurement process produced $3 million in savings in its first few months and proved easy to scale.

2. *Strategic frames* are the shared models of an uncertain situation that influence how managers and employees see the world; they include which opportunities the company will pursue (and by extension, which it will disregard), how a technology will evolve, which competitors pose the greatest threat, and which operational and financial metrics are key.[5] Standardized strategic frames ensure shared focus across the organization and minimize the odds that employees will dissipate their energy on unimportant activities. In

contrast to many Chinese entrepreneurs, who use the windfall profits from one success to diversify widely, Lu never
tired of repeating the mantra that "[w]e only do telecom,
not real estate or restaurants." Even within the telecom sector, UTStarcom maintained a standard view of how the
industry would evolve from wire line to wireless, from narrow band to broadband, and from the time division multi-
plexing protocol used by traditional voice providers to
packet switching or IP. A standardized view of how the
industry would evolve provided consistency in new product
introduction.

3. *Resources* include tangible assets such as specialized factories and land, as well as intangible assets such as brands and
technology.[6] Standardized resources confer efficiency, which
enables rapid growth. Low-cost airlines such as Southwest
Airlines and Ryanair, for example, standardize their fleets
around one plane model (such as the Boeing 737-800) to
speed turnaround times at airports and enable pilots and
crew to shift from one plane to another with ease. UTStarcom's initial focus on PAS allowed the company to rapidly
accumulate more experience with the technology, thereby
enabling more rapid installations and new product innovations than competitors could muster. Standardization also
allowed the company to build economies of scale in research
and production that reduced unit cost, allowing lower
prices to win customers.

4. *Relationships* with outside individuals and organizations—
customers, regulators, suppliers, distributors, and other
partners—provide resources critical to a start-up's success.[7]
Choices regarding relationships shape a company's internal
organization chart as well, through decisions such as which
activities to keep in-house, which to outsource, and how
business units should be organized. Some important relationships cannot be standardized, of course, such as the
friendship between Lu and Son. Standardizing high-volume

relationships, such as those with customers or partners, can minimize the costs of haggling over terms on every deal and ensure consistent quality across a variety of relationships. Franchise contracts and standardized partnership agreements are common examples of such standardization. From the beginning, UTStarcom standardized the payment terms in its contract with operators, which helped the company ramp from one customer in 1997 to over three hundred within three years.

5. *Culture* refers to the shared norms that unite and inspire employees and shape what actions they take.[8] Standardizing around the right culture can fuel employee loyalty, strengthen bonds with customers who appreciate the firm's ideology, and induce employees to do the right thing without elaborate command and control systems. Growth, however, requires new employees, and it is often difficult to maintain the desired culture during a hiring spree. UTStarcom executives recognized both the value and difficulty of standardizing their culture while moving from a few dozen employees to nearly six thousand in 2004. Chou explained that UTStarcom hired and promoted managers based on their adherence to a set of values that included goal orientation, attention to details, hard work (sixteen- to eighteen-hour days are common), and responsiveness to customer requests. Managers who embody the company's culture model the appropriate behavior and select employees below them who share the same values.

Manage Binding Constraints

Even with focus and standardization, a company can encounter constraints to the rapid growth required to seize a golden opportunity. Many of these will be minor annoyances that slow a company but do not stop it in its tracks. *Binding constraints*, in contrast, are potential bottlenecks that could prevent a company from scaling altogether.

These can come from several sources, including the management team, funding, technology evolution, or partners' ability to grow.

The first step in managing binding constraints is to know which ones matter most—a task that is neither simple nor impossible. Binding constraints are painfully obvious after they have derailed a company's growth, but by that time, of course, the damage is done. At the other end of the spectrum, worrying about every conceivable constraint that might possibly emerge in the future will dissipate management attention (and probably cause ulcers). Spotting binding constraints is easier when managers know that they should be looking for them as their company begins to scale. Lu had already scaled one business, and board members Masayoshi Son and venture capitalist Thomas Toy had scaled several. Based on their experience, they were on the lookout for barriers to growth. In UTStarcom's case, binding constraints that emerged over time included the need for cash and the management expertise required to run a larger organization.

Spotting a binding constraint is necessary, but not sufficient. Managers must also take steps to prevent such constraints from strangling growth. Part of the trick is to act when the constraint is pinching growth (signaling that it is worth worrying about) but before it brings momentum to a grinding halt. That is the time to make solving the constraint a priority for the organization. UTStarcom's founders and board, for example, identified management expertise as a possible binding constraint as the company ramped; they therefore hired seasoned executives from large companies, including Chou, as well as a vice president of engineering with twenty-nine years' experience with Lucent and a veteran chief financial officer.

Although some constraints, such as cash management, are common across companies, others are company specific and often surprising. When UTStarcom started winning contracts from local operators in the late 1990s, for example, management realized that the high price of Japanese-made handsets—which UTStarcom bought and resold at cost for $215—would dampen end-user demand for PAS systems. If end users couldn't afford the handsets, local telecommunications bureaus would not buy UTStarcom's equipment and the game would be over before it really began. UTStarcom initially tried outsourcing production to a Taiwanese company, but the contract manufacturers could only cut costs by 50 percent. Reluctantly, UT-Starcom executives decided to design and manufacture the handsets themselves in China to bring costs below the $55 to $60 price point they felt was required to ensure widespread consumer adoption. UTStarcom's continued growth also depended on continued support (or, at minimum, tolerance) of PAS from the Ministry of Information Industry. Managing this constraint required UTStarcom to devote more attention to lobbying than would be typical for many start-ups.

Hedge Against Unforeseen Problems

Even if managers do everything right, their companies will still face unanticipated challenges while ramping sales. Driving organizational change in an existing company is often compared to repairing a ship at sea. But scaling an organization is even tougher and resembles building a rocket as it is taking off—decisions must be made quickly, and mistakes can lead to crashes. Given the difficulty of the task, prudent managers will have some hedges against unforeseen contingencies. A few of the most important are as follows.

- *War chest.* Money, as the Beatles observed, can't buy you love. But a war chest of cash and marketable securities on the balance sheet can buy just about everything else. As such, it provides the perfect hedge against unexpected threats in scaling. In an uncertain world, cash in the bank can be the best investment. In the world of finance theory, capital markets are efficient, and sound companies facing temporary setbacks can raise the cash necessary to tide them over. In the real world of entrepreneurship, however, things are much more complicated. There is no guarantee that the bank till will be open when cash is needed. Sectors go in and out of fashion with investors, and funds are often unavailable when a company hits a setback. Even if the cash is gushing, it is likely to be flowing into rivals' coffers as well, thereby providing no competitive advantage. Countries such as China, moreover, lack the broad and deep capital markets required to ensure funding. Even when financing is available, the fundraising process takes time and attention, and capital raised under duress generally comes at a high price in terms of valuation, preferences, and control and may come too late to prevent a company from crashing. UTStarcom kept a healthy cushion of cash and marketable securities throughout its history and maintained access to multiple sources of funding, including venture capitalists, Softbank, corporations such as Intel, global equity, and bond markets, to top up the tank when necessary.

- *Operational and financial discipline.* Many companies sacrifice operational and financial discipline when they enter the period of hypergrowth, with the intention of growing revenues first and worrying about profits later. Instilling financial and operating discipline into a company in its early stages allows it to weather unexpected downturns, particularly price wars and higher raw material costs, and preserves the war chest. To maintain profitable growth, UTStarcom established a contract review procedure in which any contract that failed to achieve a threshold level of profitability (measured in gross margin as a percentage of sales) was rejected unless senior management explicitly approved it after careful scrutiny. The discipline of maintaining gross profit margin also prevented the company from competing on price as competitors initiated price wars. Instead, UTStarcom invested in developing a new chip set and improved manufacturing processes, which reduced handset costs and allowed the company to then cut prices without sacrificing margins.

- *Strong partners vested in your success.* One of the best ways to crash when scaling is to try to go it alone. The right partner can not only help managers anticipate possible binding constraints but also overcome them. UTStarcom actively

worked to align the interests of powerful partners to give
them an incentive to help the company overcome pockets of
turbulence as sales took off. UTStarcom executives adopted a
policy of passing on their cost savings directly to customers
and maintaining a fixed percentage gross margin on their
sales even when the company was a monopoly supplier of
PAS equipment. The resulting goodwill came in handy subsequently, as customers stayed with UTStarcom after competitors entered the market. UTStarcom's customers also worked
with the company to lobby the Ministry of Information
Industry to permit the wide deployment of PAS systems,
which was in their interest as well as UTStarcom's.

- *Owners in it for the long haul.* Even though it happens
  quickly, scaling a business can extend over several years
  before growth slows. The long duration of the scaling period
  requires an ownership and governance structure that allows
  for such long-term action and accepts that there will be
  bumps along the way. UTStarcom was fortunate to have
  investors who were in it for the long haul, including Son and
  management. Chinese state-owned enterprises, in contrast,
  run the risk that political priorities will change in midstream
  and deprive the company of resources required to scale.

- *Managers willing to take the plunge.* Managers also need to
  be sure that they themselves have the stomach to scale before
  making the leap. Accessing the resources to scale generally
  requires fundraising, and most capital providers require decision rights in exchange for funds. The bottom line is simple:
  managers must give up their autonomy in exchange for the
  resources required to get big right. Some managers prefer to
  stay small and in control rather than get big and relinquish
  their ability to run the show. Make no mistake—deciding to
  go for the gold is a gut-wrenching decision. Once a company
  starts, there is no turning back. Managers must invest in
  advance and then drive revenues to cover the resulting fixed
  costs. The virtuous circle of growth attracting the resources

to fuel future growth can flip into reverse and become a vicious cycle. If a company starts growing and stalls, potential investors, customers, employees, and partners may lose faith and may withhold the resources required to break out of the tailspin. Committing to getting big also puts a company on larger rivals' radar screens and opens it to attack. UTStarcom's Chou recalls that his first reaction to landing the first large installation in Xian in 1999 was excitement, followed quickly by panic at the prospect of crossing the Rubicon.

Summary

This chapter described some of the challenges in scaling a business to pursue a golden opportunity. It discussed things that can go wrong when everything goes right, as well as ways to manage the challenges of rapid growth. The chapter's key points are summarized in the following list. The next, and final, chapter discusses some leadership implications of managing in an unpredictable market.

- *Getting big right* refers to effectively scaling an organization to meet rapidly growing customer demand and fill a gap in the market before competitors rush in. Rapid revenue growth strains a company's resources and requires careful management. Exercising the discipline to maintain a clear focus is critical to getting big right.

- *Standardize what matters.* As companies move beyond the initial period of experimentation, ad hoc processes appropriate to the start-up phase fail under the strain of rapid growth when scaling. Managers must install standardized systems that consistently and reliably perform routine operations without top executive attention. Executives should standardize along five dimensions: key processes, strategic frames, resources, relationships, and culture.

- *Binding constraints* are potential bottlenecks that could prevent a company from scaling altogether. Some binding constraints are common across companies, including availability of funding and the top management team's ability to tackle big-company problems. Others are company specific and often surprising, emerging from idiosyncratic sources such as the relevant technology evolution or specific partners' ability to grow.

- Even if entrepreneurs carefully manage the process of getting big right, firms will still face unanticipated challenges while scaling. Prudent managers will develop *hedges against unforeseen contingencies*, including building a war chest of surplus cash, maintaining operational and financial discipline, lining up powerful partners vested in the firm's success, and ensuring that owners and the managers themselves are willing to take the plunge and stay in it for the long haul.

NINE

Leading in an Unpredictable World

THE CORE MESSAGE of this book boils down to a few sentences: in markets (such as China) where multiple, uncertain variables interact, managers enjoy limited visibility into the future. Abandoning the fiction of prediction and acknowledging the fog of the future profoundly reshape how one must think about strategy. According to the traditional view, the objective of strategy is first to build and then to protect a sustainable competitive advantage. In this approach, managers follow a linear process in which they predict which combination of position, resources, and competencies will confer future advantage; develop a plan to build the chosen advantage; and subsequently execute according to plan. In practice, of course, the process is more circuitous. Managers continually revise details of the plan, for example, and implementation encounters unmarked roadblocks. Regardless, the underlying logic of predict, plan, and implement remains intact, and so the *content* of the strategy rather than the strategic process itself ultimately creates value.

Contrast this traditional view with the unconventional perspective introduced in this book. Entrepreneurs and managers advance into the fog of the future despite sharply limited visibility of how events will unfold. Their environment produces a steady stream of modest opportunities and threats interspersed with major events. In unpredictable markets, managers can best conceptualize competition as repeated rounds of quick responses to new opportunities and emergent threats. In these circumstances, the *process* of translating situational understanding into decisive action always trumps the content of strategy. The SAPE cycle describes how managers *sense* the overall situation, *anticipate* emerging threats and opportunities, *prioritize* necessary actions, and *execute* quickly and effectively. Over time, a company that successfully outcycles its competition accumulates significant advantage.

This novel view of strategy requires fresh thinking about the role of leadership. Where established companies in stable markets can run on autopilot for many quarters with limited guidance from the figureheads in the executive suite, firms in unpredictable markets such as China need fully engaged leaders who monitor the competitive context for emerging opportunities and threats, set corporate priorities, build and maintain flexible hierarchies, and periodically declare and bet big on a main effort to pursue a golden opportunity or respond to a sudden-death threat. The following sections discuss some principles of effective leadership in an unpredictable world.

Situation Pull Versus Vision Push

Managers often equate successful leadership with crystal-clear long-term vision, often articulated in a "mission statement," or a statement of "strategic intent" or "corporate purpose," designed to anchor a company to a long-term view of what it should be doing and where it should be going.[1] Long-term visions purportedly raise expectations, point people in a shared direction, and energize them to move forward. Management gurus often cite U.S. president John F. Kennedy's committing to sending a man to the moon (and bringing him back) by the end of the decade. Kennedy's vision galvanized the nation and united diverse interests in a common goal that propelled the country ahead of the Soviet Union in the space race. Management writers often exhort executives to follow Kennedy's lead by declaring a specific, concrete vision so that they too can be great leaders.

Although leadership gurus have extolled the benefits of a long-term vision, they have downplayed the risks, which can be quite substantial in an unpredictable world. The siren song of a long-term vision can distract employees and managers from opportunities and threats emerging in the present. Long-term visions can also tempt managers to bet too much, too early. Finally, a crystal-clear long-term vision can lull employees into a false sense of security that the future is clear, when in fact it is anything but. In rapidly changing environments—not just emerging markets such as China, India, and Brazil but also technology-intensive industries and domains where different industries are converging, such as information technology, entertainment, telecommunications, and consumer electronics—a long-term vision can paralyze managers.

Most Chinese learned this lesson. When thinking about long-term vision, they recall Mao, not Kennedy. The entrepreneurs whom we studied recognized the costs of vision because most of them lived through Chairman Mao's ill-fated Great Leap Forward and Cultural Revolution. In pursuing these initiatives, Mao bet heavily on his grand vision, disregarded negative feedback, and passed up more modest opportunities; in the process, he imposed an enormous cost on his country. Mao's attempts late in his career to impose a certain vision on an uncertain future contrast with his earlier pragmatism, in which his actions were based on the facts on the ground. Recall how he disregarded the Communist International's vision of a proletariat-led communist revolution and instead adopted the rural guerrilla warfare well suited to the reality of the Chinese situation.

The stark contrast between Mao's early success while acting on a sober assessment of the situation and his later disasters while imposing a long-term vision etched itself on the psyches of the entrepreneurs we studied, who shared a healthy skepticism for grand visions. Haier Chairman Zhang explained: "Mao Zedong's magic weapon for success before the Cultural Revolution was 'seeking the truth from facts' rather than vision or dogma . . . The reason for Mao's mistakes in his old years is that he didn't abide by the principle of 'seeking the truth from facts.'"[2]

Rather than blindly following a preconceived long-term vision, managers in unpredictable markets should sense the situation in all its complexity and anticipate emerging threats and opportunities in the short to medium term. Corporate priorities, and hence action, should grow out of the situation rather than being pushed by a pre-existing vision of what should work. Qinghou Zong, for example, denies that he had any long-term vision for Wahaha. Instead, he attributes the beverage maker's success to responding to the situation: "The success of Wahaha comes from the flexible adjustment of strategy to the situation . . . I don't think that I can successfully plan long-term goals. The situation develops too fast, and the pace is so quick, it is impossible to plan for long term. It is not bad if we can plan for two to three years."

But managers should not disregard foresight altogether. In an unpredictable market, managers should adopt a fuzzy vision, such as "we aspire to be a global leader in our industry." Although such a generic vision does little more than codify the obvious, it can help executives to clarify and communicate the industry definition and the company's global scope and level of aspiration. Fuzzy visions provide the appropriate level of focus without locking a company into too narrow a course. Executives should not, however, mistake these visions for incantations endowed with the magical properties as management gurus suggest. Fuzzy visions do tell employees what industry the company is in and where it competes globally. One hopes, however, that they already get these points. Fuzzy visions do raise aspirations, but in practice, no one can distinguish such statements from competitors' versions, and so they provide no competitive advantage.

In unpredictable markets, visions are not totally irrelevant, but they are far from the essence of leadership. The right wording will not spell the difference between success and failure, and so managers should emphasize the activities that allow them to translate their understanding of the situation into appropriate action. Specifically, executives should focus on sensing the environment, anticipating emerging threats and opportunities, setting priorities, making the hard calls to execute on these priorities, and building and maintaining an organization that can make the vision a reality.

Patience Is a Virtue

Business schools often train leaders to act. But in an unpredictable market where the situation is evolving rapidly, a bias for action can lead to chasing every opportunity as if it were the chance of a lifetime or responding to every threat as if it could destroy the company. Managers must resist such temptations. Pursuing every opportunity with equal vigor dissipates an organization's focus and reserves. Active waiting requires leaders to remain calm while others are panicking. This calmness reassures the troops and conserves organizational energy, attention, and resources for those critical events that constitute true golden opportunities or sudden-death threats.

Haier's Zhang provides an excellent example of a manager who saw a great opportunity and displayed the patience to wait for the opportune moment to strike. Zhang described Haier's decision to build its industrial park, then as now the largest of its kind in China:

The idea did not come up suddenly. We had the idea earlier but the timing wasn't good, since it was rather difficult to get [a] large amount of land in the past. Even after a time-consuming application, going through all levels of the authorities to get approval, we could only gain a small piece of land. It was not until Deng Xiao-ping's South Tour in 1992 and his famous speech advocating [a] quicker pace of reform that many policies shifted. With reform going deeper the policy on land acquisition grew more lenient, and we grasped the opportunity from Deng's speech to get the land deal done because we knew the lenient land policy wouldn't last long . . . [We raised] loans from banks and bought the land to build the country's largest industrial park for electronic appliances. Less than *two months later, the government put an end to the land policy and tightened loan issuing because there were too many companies borrowing money from banks for real estate projects, causing many financial risks. Many loans which had already been approved were put to a mandatory suspension. Later, the equity market was opened [also due to Deng's advocacy during his southern tour]. Corporations could raise capital by listing their stock. Haier seized this opportunity to raise 369 million yuan [approximately $70 million at then prevailing exchange rates]. With this money, Haier built the industrial park . . . it was a question whether or not you could seize the opportunity when the time was right. At that time, many corporations ignored the opportunity or misjudged that the policy would remain open in future. The fundamental reason [why we could grasp the opportunity] was that we already had a solid foundation for future development and we did have a need for land.*

This patience requires the persistence to stay in the game while waiting for the opportune moment. Zhang's colleague Mianmian Yang used the phrase "tenacity quotient," or TQ, to describe this trait: "There are three 'Qs' necessary to succeed in China. IQ is required so a manager can correctly understand a thing. EQ so he will possess a positive attitude toward life and work with others, and TQ so he can strive over the bumps in the road and not get depressed by difficulties." Many multinational firms have failed in China because top executives lacked the tenacity to stay the course. After being attracted to the country's vast internal market and low-cost labor, they reduced their commitment when a shock threatened their subsidiary's profitability.

What If the Other Guy Is Right?

Some equate leadership with projecting certainty while others waver. Naturally, decisiveness matters when declaring and pursuing a golden opportunity or sudden-death threat. But these instances are relatively rare even in the most volatile environments—organizations spend the majority of their time actively waiting. During periods of active waiting, leaders must maintain the intellectual humility to recognize that there is much they do not and cannot know. The simple question "What if the other guy is right?" captures an important insight about the intellectual humility that leaders need when advancing into an uncertain future. In some cases a manager will know what he or she does not know. A manager might recognize, for example, that a new venture's success depends on the effectiveness of a new technology, without knowing whether that technology will work. When multiple uncertain variables interact, however, executives must also deal with what they do not know they do not know. Situations will arise that no one could have foreseen, often because of complex interactions of individually uncertain variables. Some of these unpredictable situations will pose threats, others opportunities. Success lies in responding to them.

Throughout their education and career, most people advance for what they know. They receive good grades on exams and promotions based on technical expertise. However, top executives in unpredictable environments must have the humility to recognize how much they do not know. When meeting successful Chinese entrepreneurs, one will immediately notice their humility and their fastidious listening. Recall, for instance, how Sina's founder Wang deliberately sought advice from knowledgeable venture capitalists, or how Legend founder Liu forged a joint venture with Hewlett-Packard primarily to learn rather than increase sales (although he did both in the end).

Courage to Go for the Gold

Finally, when the golden opportunity appears, a company must go for it. In the corporate setting, this involves declaring the main effort for the entire company and mobilizing whatever resources are necessary to seize the moment. Alternatively, sudden-death threats may arise that require drastic surgery. In volatile environments, you cannot avoid making these hard decisions and cannot choose their timing or form, nor will you ever have 100 percent of the information you would like. These decisions take courage. The entrepreneurs whom we interviewed all expressed a need for courage—both physical and mental—when they believed the time was right. We end this book with a reminder that above all, leadership in unpredictable markets requires courage.

Research Design
and Methodology

THIS BOOK is part of a multiyear research program I began in 1999 to explore effective strategy in unpredictable markets. The research consists of in-depth case study research to analyze how start-ups and established companies devise and execute strategies in unpredictable markets. To study this phenomenon, I selected competitive domains with high levels of uncertainty across multiple variables, including technology, macroeconomics, regulation, capital markets, and global competition. In each domain, I conducted in-depth case studies of firms that successfully managed uncertainty. Each successful firm was paired with a similar but less successful firm, and the paired case analysis was supplemented by a study of the industrial and national contexts. In addition to the Chinese cases described in this book, I studied ten Brazilian firms, enterprise software companies, medical device firms, consumer electronics companies, and airlines. (Findings from the Brazilian study can be found in a book coauthored with Martin Escobari entitled *Success Against the*

Odds: What Brazilian Champions Teach Us About Thriving in Unpredictable Markets, published by Elsevier-Campus in 2005; other findings can be found in published case studies.)

China's appeal, from my perspective, was not only the inherent interest and importance of that country's economy and recent history. More importantly, the high levels of uncertainty facing entrepreneurs provided an excellent domain for studying how firms manage in a rapidly changing and unpredictable environment. The research began in January 2003 and extended through September 2004. From the beginning, I worked closely with Yong Wang, a native of the People's Republic of China, who served as my research assistant throughout the duration of this project. At various points in the process, we were assisted by others whose roles are described in this appendix. All written data, including company archival information, trade and business press articles, books, case studies, and equity analyst reports, were collected in both English and Chinese (which was translated into English).

Selection of Industries

I decided to focus on four industries to achieve diversity of sectors while keeping the number of sectors manageable. To select the industries, we analyzed the history, performance, and nature of competition for approximately a dozen major sectors in China, relying on secondary literature in the Chinese and Western business press, published case studies, books, and reports by equity analysts, research organizations, and so forth. We also interviewed experts on the Chinese economy. We selected four sectors on which to focus our analysis: information technology, telecommunications equipment and services, food and beverages, and white goods. We chose these industries for the following reasons:

- They were among the first industries in China to integrate into global markets for products, technology, capital, and labor, and entry into the global market economy constituted a major source of uncertainty for Chinese firms.

- The industries had evolved to the point at which winners and losers had appeared. China's automobile and mobile telephone handset industries, in contrast, are also global, but it is too early in the evolution of the domestic industry to distinguish between successful and less successful firms. We are not, of course, arguing that the successful firms we have studied will maintain their position indefinitely, but only that their success to date provides valuable insights on managing in unpredictable markets.

- These industries are sufficiently large and important that credible sector and competitive data are available for them. We have reservations about the quality of financial and industry data available even for the industries we selected, but it is far better and more extensive than the data available for less prominent industries. Our four sectors also attracted significant media attention, which provided further data.

- We wanted to maintain diversity in our sample of industries. Information technology and telecommunications are relatively high tech, food and beverages low tech, and white goods somewhere in between. Telecommunications companies sell to a small set of customers (i.e., telephone service providers such as China Telecom), whereas food and beverage and white goods producers sell to the mass market through distributors. White goods has a large export component, whereas food and beverages remains a largely local business. It is, of course, impossible to achieve a perfectly representative sample of China's complex economy with only four industries, but we tried to at least introduce some variety into the industries we analyzed.

Selection of Companies Within Each Industry

Within each industry, we used a rigorous selection process to choose the companies we studied. After deciding which four industries to target, we began with a list of over sixty public and private firms across the four sectors generated through a variety of data sources, including trade publications, government reports, equity analyst reports, articles in the Chinese business press, trade association publications, and interviews with industry experts. We narrowed this to a list of approximately twenty companies based on their financial performance through the 1990s as well as company rankings by *FinanceAsia* and *Economic Observer*. To further refine our list, we surveyed prominent Chinese business academics, senior executives in Chinese firms, business journalists, and other experts for their assessment of which firms led their sectors.

This screening resulted in a list of ten to twelve companies in the four industries. During the preliminary stage, we analyzed these companies in greater depth. We collected and analyzed articles in the business press on each of these companies. We compared their operating performance (e.g., market share, new product development, quality levels) and financial metrics (e.g., revenue growth, cash flow generated, profitability, valuation for public companies) to domestic competitors and, where possible, to global leaders in the same industry. We also evaluated the firms' global competitiveness measured by their success in exports, performance on key benchmarks, or ability to withstand the entry of leading multinationals into China. We focused on cases where success was specific to the firms and not the industry—that is, the company succeeded in industries where many or most of its rivals experienced significant difficulties.

In choosing our companies, we also attempted to achieve a diversity of organizational forms, such as public and private companies, focused and diversified, and so on. Our sample of companies also covered the regional differences in China, with companies headquartered in Beijing, in the Yangtze Delta, and in the Pearl River Delta. By studying such a different group of companies, we increase our confidence that these findings are general and not idiosyncratic to a specific region, industry, or organizational form. Our final eight companies were Lenovo and Sina in information technology, UT-Starcom and AsiaInfo in telecommunications equipment and service, Haier and Galanz in white goods, and Wahaha and Ting Hsin in food and beverages.

To conduct more thorough research, we paired each of our eight focal companies with a comparable firm that was less successful in navigating China's uncertain market. These paired companies provide a valuable contrast to our more successful firms. The similarities among these companies, as well as the differences between them and their less-successful peers, form the foundation for our findings.

Data Collection and Analysis

We began our in-depth analysis of our eight companies by collecting data from multiple public sources and creating a detailed timeline averaging several hundred key events per company. Teams of analysts in Beijing and Shanghai collected and analyzed public data in Chinese and English in several categories, including financial performance, technology, and key partnerships. Two local Chinese consulting firms, E. J. McKay in Shanghai and Sinotrust Consulting in Beijing, hired and managed these teams under our supervision. A team of six analysts was employed full-time for the summer of 2003 on this project, and another four analysts were employed on a part-time basis for a longer period to support the project. The resulting chronology of company events, financial and operating analyses, and company profiles provided the basis for structuring interview questions. At this point, we also selected paired firms that were less successful to compare with our firms and began gathering comparable data for them.

After collecting and analyzing these public data, we conducted several dozen in-depth face-to-face interviews over a monthlong period, supplementing these with phone and e-mail interviews. The typical face-to-face interview lasted at least an hour, although most were two hours to accommodate the time required to translate. All interviews consisted of at least two interviewers, and most also included a third party to act as translator and a fourth to take notes in both Chinese and English. We interviewed senior executives, middle managers, and board members of the more successful companies, and when possible the paired company as well. The majority of interviews were conducted in Chinese and simultaneously translated into

English. All interviews were tape recorded, and key tapes were transcribed. Transcripts were checked for accuracy against all interviewers' notes, and discrepancies or errors were analyzed and corrected. During these interviews we also requested and received relevant internal records from the company's archives, which were subsequently translated into English and analyzed. In addition, we made extensive use of e-mail interviews, in which interviewees responded to our questions in writing and used their own staff to translate the Chinese into English.

After the interviews, we wrote descriptive case studies of each of the companies in our sample; these cases formed the basis for the company histories in this book. We collected additional data and conducted more interviews at this stage to clarify things that we did not understand and to fill gaps in the data. In addition, I supervised ten students (all second-year MBA students at the Harvard Business School and all natives of the People's Republic of China) who worked in teams to research and write in-depth teaching case studies on five of the eight companies in our sample. In the course of their research, the student teams conducted additional interviews and collected supplementary company and industry data, which they translated for inclusion in the teaching case studies. These case studies consisted of approximately twenty pages of single-spaced text and an additional twenty pages of exhibits. We validated our findings by reviewing the case studies with senior executives in the companies to ensure the accuracy of facts and that no confidential data had inadvertently been disclosed. At this point, we also conducted a final round of interviews with the entrepreneurs and senior executives in the companies to address additional questions that had emerged during the research.

CHAPTER ONE

1. An Amazon.com search conducted on November 25, 2004, produced over 130 books on Henry Ford and over fifty on Bill Gates alone. The search was limited to books with the entrepreneur's name in the title field.

2. Data was drawn from State Statistical Bureau of the People's Republic of China, *China Statistical Yearbook* (Beijing: State Statistical Bureau of the People's Republic of China, 2003); and Central Intelligence Agency, *The World Factbook* (Washington, DC: GPO, 2004).

3. Dominic Wilson and Roopa Purushothaman, "Dreaming with BRICs: The Path to 2050," Goldman Sachs report, October 2003, 5.

4. Economist Intelligence Unit, *Coming of Age: Multinational Companies in China* (London: The Economist Intelligence Unit, 2004).

5. Wu Yan, "State Council's No. 10 Decree Won Acclaim Among Real Estate Developers," *Economic Reference*, September 2, 2003.

6. "National Beverage Policy Might Be Adjusted," *China Securities Daily*, December 9, 2002.

7. "Negotiations Between Chinese DVD Manufacturers and 6C Alliance," *Nanfang Dushi Daily*, May 15, 2002.

8. See Kellee S. Tsai, *Back Alley Banking: Private Entrepreneurs in China* (Ithaca, NY: Cornell University Press, 2002).

9. For initial findings from this research program, see Donald N. Sull, "Disciplined Entrepreneurship," *MIT Sloan Management Review* 46, no. 1 (2004): 71–77; Donald N. Sull and Martin Escobari, "Creating Value in an Unpredictable World," *Business Strategy Review* 15, no. 3 (2004): 14–20;

Kathleen M. Eisenhardt and Donald N. Sull, "Strategy as Simple Rules," *Harvard Business Review* 79, no. 1 (2001): 107–116; and a series of published case studies, including BEA Systems and Siebel Systems (enterprise software), Emirates Airline and easyJet (airlines), Companhia Cervejaria Brahma, America Latina Logistica, Natura and Weg (Brazil), AsiaInfo and UTStarcom (Chinese telecommunications) and Conor Medsystems (medical devices).

10. Donald N. Sull and Martin Escobari, *Success Against the Odds: What Brazilian Champions Teach Us About Thriving in Unpredictable Markets* (London and São Paulo: Elsevier/Campus, 2005).

11. We are extremely grateful to several experts on Chinese history and economics who graciously took the time to review our summary of recent Chinese history, particularly Professor Laixiang Sun of the School of Oriental and African Studies (SOAS), University of London; Dr. Dic Lo, also of SOAS; and Professor Lin Xu of Babson College.

12. Excellent treatments of modern China include Kenneth Lieberthal, *Governing China from Revolution to Reform*, 2nd ed. (New York: W. W. Norton, 2003); Robert Kennedy, "China Facing the 21st Century," Case 798-066 (Boston: Harvard Business School, 2002); Graham Hutchings, *Modern China* (Cambridge, MA: Harvard University Press, 2001); Jonathan Spence, *The Search for Modern China* (New York: W. W. Norton, 1990); Bruce Scott and Jamie Matthews, "China's Rural Leap Forward," Case 703-024 (Boston: Harvard Business School, 2003); Jonathan Woetzel, *Capitalist China* (Singapore: John Wiley & Sons, 2003); John Bryan Starr, *Understanding China* (New York: Hill and Wang, 1997); and Yasheng Huang, *Selling China: Foreign Direct Investment During the Reform Era* (New York: Cambridge University Press, 2003).

13. Angus Maddison, *Monitoring the World Economy, 1820–1992* (Paris: OECD, 1995).

14. The famine is also estimated to have resulted in over 30 million postponed births in the years between 1958 and 1961. See B. Ashtone, K. Hill, A. Piazza, and R. Zeitz, "Famine in China, 1958–61," *Population and Development Review* 10, no. 4 (1984): 613–645. The number of people who died directly from the resulting famine as well as the postponed births are typically estimated by comparing actual population figures with projections of population growth based on historical trends. These figures, as a result, should be interpreted as approximate estimates rather than precise figures. I thank Dr. Dic Lo of the School of Oriental and African Studies for this observation.

15. I am deeply indebted to Professor Laixiang Sun and Dr. Lo of the School of Oriental and African Studies, University of London, who pointed

out how the economic decentralization instituted during the Cultural Revolution helped lay the groundwork for China's subsequent economic development. China's licensing of Japanese technology in the 1970s, to cite one often overlooked example, was an early experiment in integrating China into the global economy.

16. L. Putterman, "On the Past and Future of China's Township and Village Enterprises," *World Development* 25, no. 10 (1997): 1639–1655.

17. Scott and Matthews, "China's Rural Leap Forward."

18. Ibid.

19. Woetzel, *Capitalist China*.

20. *The Columbia Electronic Encyclopedia*, 6th ed. (New York: Columbia University Press, 2004).

CHAPTER TWO

1. Sources on Sina Corporation include interviews with company executives; company documents; and secondary sources such as filings with the Securities and Exchange Commission, articles in the Chinese business press, and equity analyst reports.

2. Based on a survey of more than two thousand Chinese Internet users conducted by the Chinese Academy of Social Sciences in 2003. Twenty-nine percent of users surveyed listed Sina as their most-visited site, versus 18 percent who listed Sohu as their favorite Web site. Nearly two-thirds of those surveyed listed Sina as among their top three most-visited Web sites. See Chinese Academy of Social Sciences, *Report on Internet Usage and Impact on Twelve Chinese Cities* (Beijing: Chinese Academy of Social Sciences, 2003).

3. See Mary Meeker, Lina Choi, and Yoshiko Motoyama, *The China Internet Report*, Morgan Stanley equity research report, April 14, 2004, http://www.morganstanley.com/institutional/techresearch/2004_China_Report.html.

4. Xiaomin Wang, "Zhongguancun Science Park: A SWOT Analysis," Visiting Researchers Series no. 10 (Singapore: Institute of Southeast Asian Studies, 2000). See also the Zhongguancun Science Park website (http://www.zhongguancun.com.cn/en/).

5. The end of the fiscal year for Sina Corporation and its predecessor entity Beijing Stone Rich Sight Information Company was June until 2003, when the company switched its fiscal year to the calendar year. For the sake of consistency, all financial data reported in this chapter are for a fiscal year ending in June, unless otherwise noted.

6. Ronald Chan, *Sina.com: Leading Internet Play in China*, Dresdner Kleinwort Benson equity research report, September 14, 2000, 26. Although

this estimate of 2004 advertising revenues was high, it was not out of line with those of other analysts, who forecast revenues of $80 to $90 million for Sina.com in that same year.

7. *Asiaweek* ("Out of the Frying Pan," September 28, 2001), for example, wrote: "The deal smacks of desperation because possible synergies in broadband content provision still seem a long way off. 'They haven't really clearly identified their strategy at this point,' says Matthew McGarvey, a Beijing-based analyst at tech research firm IDC. Sun and Sina investors will be hoping that the companies don't go down in flames together."

8. Strategy and organizational scholars have used different terms to describe unpredictable markets, including "turbulence," "high velocity," "hypercompetition," "revolution," and "chaos." See F. Emery and E. Trist, "The Causal Texture of Organizational Environments," *Human Relations* 18 (1965): 21–32; L. J. Bourgeois and K. M. Eisenhardt, "Strategic Decision Processes in High-Velocity Environments: Four Cases in the Microcomputer Industry," *Management Science* 34, no. 7 (1988): 816; R. A. D'Aveni, *Hypercompetition: Managing the Dynamics of Strategic Maneuvering* (New York: Free Press, 1994); G. Hamel, *Leading the Revolution* (Boston: Harvard Business School Press, 2000); and T. J. Peters, *Thriving on Chaos: Handbook for a Management Revolution* (New York: Knopf, 1987). All of these constructs emphasize complexity (i.e., multiple factors) and dynamism (i.e., the rate of change of variables), and several discuss interactions as well. I use the term *unpredictability* to simplify rather than complicate this terminological proliferation. From a manager's perspective, the critical implication of complexity, dynamism, and interaction is the difficulty of predicting what the future holds. Thus, *unpredictability* is a simple word that goes to the essence of the managerial challenge. The phrase *the fog of the future* is intended as a vivid visual metaphor of this unpredictability.

9. Military theorists have thought systematically about the role of time and timing in unpredictable environments, and I draw on many of their insights in my model. Clausewitz introduced several important temporal constructs in addition to the fog of war, including "culminating points" (time for decisive action) and "pauses" (temporary lulls between intense conflict). See Karl von Clausewitz, *On War*, trans. M. Howard and P. Paret (Princeton, NJ: Princeton University Press, 1984).

10. See D'Aveni, *Hypercompetition*, and Hamel, *Leading the Revolution,* for a representative sample of arguments that the global economy is growing less predictable. There has been surprisingly little empirical research testing this hypothesis, and findings from the existing research offer mixed evidence on whether the economy as a whole has become more

volatile, at least in the United States. For findings supporting increased volatility, see L. G. Thomas, "The Two Faces of Competition: Dynamic Resourcefulness and the Hypercompetitive Environment," *Organization Science* 7 (1996): 221–242. For conflicting findings, see G. McNamara, P. M. Vaaler, and C. Devers, "Same As It Ever Was: The Search for Evidence of Increasing Hypercompetition," *Strategic Management Journal* 24 (2003): 261–278.

11. See Donald N. Sull, "Disciplined Entrepreneurship," *MIT Sloan Management Review* 46, no. 1 (2004); and Donald N. Sull and Martin Escobari, "Creating Value in an Unpredictable World," *Business Strategy Review* 15, no. 3 (2004): 14–20.

12. For an in-depth discussion of how firms create and sustain value in unpredictable markets, see Sull and Escobari, "Creating Value in an Unpredictable World."

13. The importance of selecting an industry position is most closely associated with Michael Porter. See Michael Porter, *Competitive Strategy: Techniques for Analyzing Industries and Competitors* (New York: Free Press, 1980) and *Competitive Advantage: Creating and Sustaining Superior Performance* (New York: Free Press, 1985). Recent empirical studies suggest that stable industry effects account for approximately 19 percent of the differences in profitability among U.S. public corporations. See A. McGahan and M. E. Porter, "How Much Does Industry Matter, Really?" *Strategic Management Journal* 18 (Summer special issue, 1997): 15–30; and R. Schmalensee, "Do Markets Differ Much?" *American Economic Review* 75, no. 3 (1985): 341–351. Using a different methodology, Rumelt estimates industry effects as only 8 percent, but this lower estimate may result from his exclusive focus on manufacturing industries. See R. Rumelt, "How Much Does Industry Matter?" *Strategic Management Journal* 12, no. 3 (1991): 167–185. It is important to note, however, that all of these studies were conducted in the United States at a time when the industries were already mature. In the earlier stages of industrial development, comparable to China's current situation, the correlation between industry and profitability may be weaker. U.S. industries that are unprofitable in their current state of maturity (e.g., steel, tires, basic chemicals, railways) were quite attractive in their initial decades. The specifics of the Chinese context may alter the relative attractiveness of industries compared with Western markets. China's current construction boom, for example, may allow steel mills to earn outsized profits, whereas the high costs of basic research and uncertain intellectual property rights make pharmaceuticals a much less profitable industry in China than in the United States or Europe.

14. B. Wernerfelt, "A Resource-Based View of the Firm," *Strategic Management Journal* 5, no. 2 (1984): 171–180; and J. Barney, "Firm Resources and Sustained Competitive Advantage," *Journal of Management* 17, no. 1 (1991): 99–120.

15. Gary Hamel and C. K. Prahalad introduced the concept of the core competence of the firm. See G. Hamel and C. K. Prahalad, "The Core Competence of the Corporation," *Harvard Business Review*, May–June 1990.

16. Pankaj Ghemawat argues that strategy consists of making commitments or infrequent large changes in resources that have large and enduring effects on a company's future alternatives. See P. Ghemawat, *Commitment* (New York: Free Press, 1991). The importance of these decisions implies that managers very clearly analyze their consequences long into the future. Ghemawat's argument hinges on the assumption that managers have sufficient visibility into the future to analyze the consequences of their actions, although he of course admits the presence of uncertainty. Although other scholars have been less explicit in asserting the possibility of prediction, they have tacitly assumed visibility in their models. Both the position and competency views assume that managers can predict ex ante which industry will be attractive in the future and which resources valuable. These assumptions are, of course, quite valid in stable markets but less so in unpredictable markets.

An alternative perspective holds that managers make their best estimate on the optimal future strategy based on the data at hand. Bounds on managers' information processing capability, coupled with environmental unpredictability, however, severely limit managers' ability to predict the outcomes of their actions. See R. Amit and P. J. H. Schoemaker, "Strategic Assets and Organizational Rent," *Strategic Management Journal* 4 (1993): 33–46. This view implies that developing and deploying resources or staking out an apparently attractive market position is essentially like buying a lottery ticket, and the authors themselves acknowledge that their view logically precludes the development of a theory that could help guide managers' actions.

I believe that management theory should provide normative guidance to managers rather than simply explain variance in performance after the fact. As a result, I focus my attention on the stream of strategy research that offers advice to managers in addition to description or prediction.

17. Paul Goodman and associates note the surprising lack of explicit attention paid to temporal constructs in organization and strategy theory. See P. S. Goodman, B. S. Lawrence, D. G. Ancona, and M. T. Tushman, "Introduction to Special Topic Forum on Time and Organization Research," *Academy of Management Review* 26, no. 4 (2001): 507–511. Deeply embedded assumptions, however, are often the most difficult to surface and

analyze; thus, the relative paucity of research to date most likely testifies to the importance of time as a construct.

18. A concrete example of extrapolation occurs in the financial models used to value the cash flows produced by established businesses. These models isolate key variables, take their historical values as a base case, and extrapolate future cash flows based on incremental changes to these variables. See, for example, T. Copeland, T. Koller, and J. Murrin, *Valuation: Measuring and Managing the Value of Companies* (New York: John Wiley, 1996), especially pp. 133–324.

19. Meyer models "environmental jolts" as inherently transient events preceded and followed by equilibrium. See A. D. Meyer, "Adapting to Environmental Jolts," *Administrative Science Quarterly* 27 (1982): 434. This is consistent with a broad body of research that models systems as experiencing long periods of stability punctuated by brief and infrequent periods of systemic change. See M. Tushman and E. Romanelli, "Organizational Evolution: A Metamorphosis Model of Convergence and Reorientation," in *Research in Organizational Behavior* 7, eds. L. L. Cummings and B. M. Staw (Greenwich, CT: JAI Press, 1985), 171–222.

20. Organization and strategy scholars have recently begun to examine alternative concepts of time explicitly. See, for example, D. G. Ancona, G. A. Okhuysen, and L. A. Perlow, "Taking Time to Integrate Temporal Research," *Academy of Management Review* 26, no. 4 (2001): 512–529.

21. More precisely, changes in complex systems frequently follow some version of a power law in which the frequency of an event's occurrence is inversely related to its magnitude. See P. Anderson, "Complexity Theory and Organization Science," *Organization Science* 10, no. 3 (1999): 223.

22. See D. J. Collis, "Research Note: How Valuable Are Organizational Capabilities?" *Strategic Management Journal* 15 (1994): 143–152.

CHAPTER THREE

1. Sources on Tingyi include interviews with company executives, company documents, and secondary sources. We are particularly grateful to Aaron Wen and Nelson Liu, both Harvard MBAs of the class of 2004, who, along with Harry Wang, wrote an unpublished, analytic case study of Ting Hsin. We are also grateful to Sheree Chuang of Commonwealth Publishing, who conducted in-depth research into Ting Hsin and Uni-President and generously made introductions to the companies and shared her insights with us.

2. At year-end 2003, the Ting Hsin Group owned only 33 percent of the equity in Tingyi, with the Japanese food company Sanyo owning an

equal stake and the remainder floated on the Hong Kong stock exchange. Despite owning only one-third of the equity in Tingyi, the Ting Hsin Group and the founding Wei family exercised effective management control over Tingyi. As of December 2003, only one of Tingyi's twelve top executives came from Sanyo, while the other eleven were hired by the Wei family. Ting Hsin cofounder Ing-Chou Wei served as chairman and chief executive officer of Tingyi. Most of the case history discussed in this chapter preceded Ting Hsin's creation of the Tingyi subsidiary, its flotation in Hong Kong in 1996, and sale of a 33 percent equity stake in Tingyi to Sanyo in 1999. To avoid unnecessary confusion, we use *Ting Hsin* throughout this chapter to refer to businesses controlled by the Wei brothers, including their operations exercised through the Tingyi Company.

3. For brief history of the noodle, see (http://www.inmamaskitchen.com/FOOD_IS_ART/pasta/historypasta.html).

4. Market share data are from AC Nielsen SCAN TRACK, for the period December 2003 to January 2004. Master Kong's high share of market measured by share compared with volume market share results from a focus on the high end of the market.

5. Alfred Grey, *Warfighting* (Washington, DC: United States Marine Corps, 1989).

6. Professor Kathleen Eisenhardt of Stanford University has identified several concrete steps that managers can take to increase the effectiveness of decision making in what she calls high-velocity environments, including gathering real-time information, considering multiple simultaneous alternatives, actively seeking the advice of outside experts, adopting decision rules to reach consensus, and integrating decisions over time. See K. M. Eisenhardt, "Making Fast Strategic Decisions in High-Velocity Environments," *Academy of Management Journal* 32, no. 3 (1989): 543–576; L. J. Bourgeois and K. M. Eisenhardt, "Strategic Decision Processes in High-Velocity Environments: Four Cases in the Microcomputer Industry," *Management Science* 34, no. 7 (1988): 816–835; and S. L. Brown and K. M. Eisenhardt, "The Art of Continuous Change: Linking Complexity Theory and Time-Paced Evolution in Relentlessly Shifting Organizations," *Administrative Science Quarterly* 42 (1997): 1–34.

7. Peter Drucker lists the unexpected and incongruities as the first two sources of opportunities. See P. F. Drucker, *Innovation and Entrepreneurship* (New York: Harper Business, 1985), 37–129.

8. Since Fredrick W. Taylor published his classic *Principles of Scientific Management* in 1911, much of Western management thinking has aimed at transforming management from an art into a science. A central tenet of this

program has been replacing managers' intuition—viewed as unreliable and idiosyncratic—with rational analysis. A milestone on the road from art to science is Chester Barnard's *The Functions of the Executive* (Cambridge, MA: Harvard University Press, 1968), which lays out a highly rational and systematic approach to management. What many people overlook when reading Barnard is his emphasis on intuition in decision making. In a speech to the faculty and students of Princeton's engineering school (recorded in an appendix to his book), Barnard argued: "Too much reasoning inhibits the intuitional processes . . . [which are] generally indispensable and more reliable in many circumstances. Habitual analysis, in other words, may teach more about a thing, but may at the same time destroy the sense of the thing as a whole." Barnard's message must have come as quite a shock to his audience, in part because they were engineers trained to approach problems logically and analytically, but also because the speaker was a senior executive at AT&T, a company known for its rational management.

9. For a more detailed discussion of designing and running experiments, see Donald N. Sull, "Disciplined Entrepreneurship," *MIT Sloan Management Review* 46, no. 1 (2004): 71–77.

CHAPTER FOUR

1. Primary data sources for Legend and Great Wall include interviews with corporate executives and corporate documents. I am also grateful to my former student Greg Ye and his coauthors (all Harvard MBAs from the class of 2001) for use of the in-depth study of Legend's response to the entry of multinational computer companies documented in Henry Chen, Harry Qin, Greg Ye, Zheng Yin, and Michael Rukstad, "A Technology Legend in China," Case 701-052 (Boston: Harvard Business School, 2001). In addition to an extensive literature review of historical articles on Legend, two secondary sources were particularly useful: Huijiang Zhu, *15 Years of Legend Group* [in Chinese] (Beijing: China CAAC Publishing House, 2002), and Qiwen Lu, *China's Leap into the Information Age: Innovation and Organization in the Computer Industry* (Oxford: Oxford University Press, 2000).

2. Market share data from International Data Corporation (IDC) for fourth quarter 2003.

3. Chen, Qin, Ye, Yin, and Rukstad, "A Technology Legend in China."

4. Darrell Rigby, "Management Tools Survey 2003: Usage Up as Companies Strive to Make Headway in Tough Times," *Strategy & Leadership* 31, no. 5 (2003): 4–11. The 2002 survey included 708 respondent firms from around the world, with approximately 20 percent from the Asia Pacific region. Bain has conducted this survey for nine consecutive years and

consistently found strategic planning processes to be the most frequently used tool over that time period.

5. To be fair, it is difficult to assess the linkage between planning processes and firm performance because much of the previous research has been limited by flaws in research design, including overly simplistic categories (e.g., "planners" versus "non-planners"), inconsistent definition of key variables, tenuous links to theory, failure to control for mediating variables, overreliance on survey data, and varied sources of data. More recent attempts to sort out the effects of strategic planning on firm-level performance using meta-analytic techniques have suggested that previous studies may have underestimated the impact. These recent studies, however, are limited by the variability and poor design of previous studies. The computer science dictum of "garbage in, garbage out" applies as much to meta-analysis as it does to computation. For recent reviews, see Thomas C. Powell, "Strategic Planning as Competitive Advantage," *Strategic Management Journal* 13, no. 7 (1992): 551–558; and C. Chet Miller and Laura B. Cardinal, "Strategic Planning and Firm Performance: A Synthesis of More Than Two Decades of Research," *Academy of Management Journal* 37, no. 6 (1994): 1649–1665. Despite the methodological limits of earlier studies, the sheer volume should have discovered a linkage between formal planning and performance if such a robust linkage existed. The failure to find a clear linkage after twenty-five years of searching suggests that it is tenuous at best.

6. Based on a comparative case study of the strategic planning process in eight of the ten largest oil and gas companies, Robert Grant found that few major decisions resulted from the formal strategic planning process. See Robert M. Grant, "Strategic Planning in a Turbulent Environment: Evidence from the Oil Majors," *Strategic Management Journal* 24, no. 6 (2003): 491–517. Another study of the impact of the formal planning process on 1,087 strategic decisions made by 129 *Fortune* 500 companies between 1982 and 1986 found that only global expansion decisions (and to a lesser degree divestment choices) were driven by the formal planning process. Other decisions, including those involving technology, acquisitions, capacity expansion, new products, strategic alliances, and organizational changes, were not influenced by the formal planning process in either their formulation or implementation. See Deepak K. Sinha, "The Contribution of Formal Planning to Decisions," *Strategic Management Journal* 11, no. 6 (1990): 479–492.

7. W. S. Lind, *Maneuver Warfare Handbook* (Boulder, CO: Westview Press, 1985), and R. Coram, *Boyd: The Fighter Pilot Who Changed the Art of War* (Boston: Little, Brown, 2002).

CHAPTER FIVE

1. Data on Haier comes from interviews with company executives. We are particularly grateful to Haier president Mianmian Yang and chairman Ruimin Zhang for being so generous with their time. The Haier history has been covered in great detail by the Chinese business press, and we drew on multiple sources as background. For an accessible history of the company in English, see Jinsheng Yi and Xian Ye, *The Haier Way: The Making of a Chinese Business Leader and a Global Brand* (Dumont, NY: Homa and Sekey Books, 2003).

2. Note that these figures for the Haier Group's revenues are self-reported. Although the company has a subsidiary, Qingdao Haier, listed on the Shanghai stock exchange, the public subsidiary accounts for only 16 percent of reported group revenue. As a result, it is difficult to evaluate the quality of the group's self-reported financials without understanding the reporting conventions employed. Given the lack of transparency in financial reporting, we are not fully confident that these numbers provide an accurate picture of the company's sales growth, particularly since we do not understand the conventions used to book sales across divisions. Despite our unease with the reported numbers, it is certainly the case that the company has increased revenues dramatically over the past two decades. How they have financed that growth and the level of underlying profitability, however, remain unclear.

3. Please see the "2004 World's Most Respected Companies Survey," by Financial Times/PricewaterhouseCoopers, *Financial Times,* November 19th, 2004. For full report, please go to http://www.pwc.com/Extweb/ncsurvres.nsf/docid/58D9F6C6C7B817BC80256F4F003FDEA1. The result is based on an annual survey of more than one thousand CEOs from twenty-five countries, as well as fund managers, media commentators, and representatives from nongovernmental organizations.

4. "World's 30 Most Respected Entrepreneurs," *Financial Times*, December 7, 1999; "2003 Most Powerful People in Business," *Fortune*, August 11, 2003.

5. The Qingdao Refrigerator Company was subsequently renamed Qingdao Haier.

6. For a fuller discussion of how Haier and other emerging-market companies innovate despite limited resources, see Donald N. Sull and Alejandro Ruelas-Gossi, "The Art of Innovating on a Shoestring," *Financial Times Mastering Innovation*, September 24, 2004.

7. See Karl E. Weick, "Educational Organizations as Loosely Coupled Systems," *Administrative Science Quarterly* 21 (1976): 1–19; and J. D.

Orton and Karl E. Weick, "Loosely Coupled Systems: A Reconceptualization," *Academy of Management Review* 15, no. 2 (1990): 203–223.

8. See Thomas R. Eisenmann, "The Effects of CEO Equity Ownership and Diversification on Risk Taking," *Strategic Management Journal* 23 (2002): 513–534.

9. See Donald N. Sull, "No Exit: The Failure of Bottom-up Processes and the Role of Top-down Disinvestment" and "Process Breakdown: A Note on the Sources and Consequences of the Failure of the Resource Allocation Process Within Established Firms," both in *Readings in the Resource Allocation Process*, eds. Joseph L. Bower and Clark Gilbert (New York: Oxford University Press, 2005).

10. Research to date has argued that top executives will tend to centralize decision making and control when an organization faces a threat but not an opportunity. See Dutton and Jackson, op. cit. Jane E. Dutton and Susan E. Jackson (1987), "Categorizing strategic issues: Links to organizational action," *Academy of Management Review* 12 (1): pp 76–90; and B. M. Staw, L. E. Sandelands, and J. E. Dutton, "Threat Rigidity Effects in Organizational Behavior: A Multi-level Analysis," *Organizational Science Quarterly* 26 (1981): 501–524. We believe that top executives will also centralize resource allocation when seizing an opportunity to the extent it (1) is of sufficient magnitude that only top management could marshal the resources to execute (e.g., major acquisition), (2) requires removal of resources from other deployments, or (3) requires more rapid action than could be expected from the existing bottom-up process. Golden opportunities, by definition, meet the first criterion; based on our empirical research they generally meet the other two as well.

11. Peter Drucker, *The Practice of Management* (New York: Harper-Collins, 1954).

12. Michael Jensen has argued persuasively for colocating decision rights with specific knowledge within a firm. See M. C. Jensen, *Theory of the Firm: Governance, Residual Claims and Organizational Forms* (Cambridge, MA: Harvard University Press, 2000).

13. I am deeply indebted to Charles Spinosa for reviewing this chapter and adding his insights, particularly on the importance of system design in enabling a flexible hierarchy.

CHAPTER SIX

1. See Jeffrey Pfeffer and Gerald R. Salancik, *The External Control of Organizations* (New York: Harper & Row, 1978).

2. Data on Galanz is from interviews with company executives, plant tours, and company documents. We are also grateful for insights from discussions with Zhang Xi, Soo Chuen Tan, and Seth Wheeler (all Harvard Business School MBAs of the class of 2004), who conducted research on the microwave oven industry. Useful secondary sources included Dehai Deng and Jian Zhou, *Made in Galanz: A Miracle Story* (Beijing: Jiangxi Renmin Publishing House, 2004), and Xuebao Song, "Guangdong Galanz: What New Marketing Strategy Should Galanz Adopt?" Case 105 (Beijing: Tsinghua University School of Economics and Management, 1999).

3. Access Asia, *Microwave Ovens in China: A Market Analysis* (Shanghai: Access Asia, 2003).

4. Xuebao Song, "Guangdong Galanz: What New Marketing Strategy Should Galanz Adopt?"

5. Average retail price per microwave sold fell from 3,000 to 4,000 RMB in the early 1990s to 447 to 503 RMB in the period 1997 through 1999. See Access Asia, *White Goods in China: A Market Analysis* (Shanghai: Access Asia, 2003), table 1:11, p. 47, for retail prices, and Access Asia, *Microwave Ovens*, table 1:5, p. 10.

6. For the history of the relationship between Ford and Firestone, see D. N. Sull, "The Dynamics of Standing Still: Firestone Tire & Rubber and the Radial Revolution," *Business History Review* 73, no. 3 (Autumn 1999): 430–464.

7. For a brief overview of the business development function in technology-intensive firms, see D. N. Sull, "Success Flows from Business Development," *Financial Times Mastering Management*, January 18, 2001.

8. Professor Howard H. Stevenson, the intellectual leader of entrepreneurship studies at the Harvard Business School, includes the absence of resources in his definition of entrepreneurship as "the pursuit of opportunity without regard to resources currently controlled." See H. H. Stevenson and D. E. Gumpert, "The Heart of Entrepreneurship," *Harvard Business Review*, March–April 1985, 2–11; and H. H. Stevenson and J. C. Jarillo-Mossi, "A Paradigm of Entrepreneurship: Entrepreneurial Management," *Strategic Management Journal* 11 (1990): 17–27.

9. For a fuller discussion of how relationships can become shackles, see chapters 1 through 3 of Donald N. Sull, *Why Good Companies Go Bad* (Boston: Harvard Business School Press, 2005).

10. Ibid.

11. There will, of course, be exceptions in industries deemed critical to the national interest, such as banking and defense suppliers. It goes without

saying that every Chinese executive must continue to keep abreast of the political situation, even if it forges partnerships with global firms.

12. The large overhang of state-owned shares on the Shanghai and Shenzhen equity markets prevents shares traded there from reflecting changes in the underlying vitality of listed businesses.

13. Donald N. Sull and Martin Escobari, *Success Against the Odds: What Brazilian Champions Teach Us About Thriving in Unpredictable Markets* (London and Sao Paulo: Elsevier/Campus, 2005). All quotations in the sidebar come from the interviews conducted for this book.

14. PricewaterhouseCoopers conducted a survey of thirty-five countries in 2001 to measure their "opacity index"—the inverse of transparency. This index measures the effects of unclear legal systems and regulations, tax policies, accounting standards and practices, and corruption on firms' ability to raise capital. See J. R. Barth et al., *The Opacity Index* (New York: PricewaterhouseCoopers Endowment for the Study of Transparency and Sustainability, 2001).

CHAPTER SEVEN

1. Data on Wahaha comes from interviews with senior executives, company records, and the Wahaha unpublished, analytical case study written by Zhang Ying, Jin Liyang, and Yuan Yong, all Harvard Business School MBAs of the class of 2004 (to be published by London Business School in 2005). Useful secondary sources in Chinese included Xiaobo Wu and Hongwei Hu, *Extreme Marketing* (Beijing: Zhejiang Renmin Publishing, 2002); Bangjue Chen, "The Secret Sales Strategy of Wahaha," *Win Weekly* [Taipei], issue 372, 2004; and Hongmin Yuan, "The Last Magnate in Beverage Business," *Global Entrepreneur Magazine* [Beijing], July 2004. A useful English case study on Wahaha's entry into the carbonated beverages sector is N. Dai and N. Dawar, "Cola Wars in China: The Future Is Here," Case 9B03A006 (London, Ontario: Richard Ivey School of Business, 2003).

2. Access Asia, *Soft Drinks in China: A Market Analysis* (Shanghai: Access Asia, 2003).

3. Correspondence between Simon Israel and author, 7 October 2004.

4. Whether a golden opportunity results in a sustainable competitive advantage depends on the duration of the period when profits exceed the cost of capital.

5. Constantinos C. Markides and Paul A. Geroski, *Fast Second: How Smart Companies Bypass Radical Innovation to Enter and Dominate New Markets* (San Francisco: Jossey-Bass, 2005).

6. Sun Tzu, *The Art of War*, trans. Lionel Giles (Mineola, NY: Dover Publications, 2002).

7. In an extensive study of newspapers' responses to the Internet, Clark Gilbert found that executives were more likely to allocate resources to the Internet when it was seen as a threat to their core business. Ironically, when executives framed the Internet as a threat to the core business rather than an opportunity, they failed to pursue the upside opportunity aggressively and concentrated on defending their core. See C. Gilbert, "Change in the Presence of Residual Fit: Can Competing Frames Coexist?" unnumbered working paper, Harvard Business School, Boston, 2004.

8. C. Christensen, *The Innovator's Dilemma* (Boston: Harvard Business School Press, 1996).

CHAPTER EIGHT

1. Data on UTStarcom comes from interviews with senior executives, company records, and the unpublished, analytical case study written by Jason Hu, Charles Xu, Allen Qian, and Julia Zheng, all Harvard Business School MBAs of the class of 2004 (to be published by London Business School in 2005).

2. For a discussion of entrepreneurship as a process of iterative experimentation, see Donald N. Sull, "Disciplined Entrepreneurship," *MIT Sloan Management Review* 46, no. 1 (2004): 71–77.

3. For a complete discussion of these elements and how actions taken early in an organization's history shape subsequent success and failure, see Donald N. Sull, *Why Good Companies Go Bad* (Boston: Harvard Business School Press, 2005), chapter 2; and Donald N. Sull, "Managing by Commitments," *Harvard Business Review*, May 2003.

4. For a comprehensive discussion of the benefits of routinization of organizational processes, see Richard R. Nelson and Sidney G. Winter, *An Evolutionary Theory of Economic Change* (Cambridge, MA: Belknap, 1982), 96–136. For a useful taxonomy of processes from a managerial perspective, see David A. Garvin, "The Processes of Organization and Management," *MIT Sloan Management Review* 39, no. 4 (1998): 33–50.

5. For a thorough discussion of how shared strategic frames shape organizational performance, see Joseph F. Porac, Howard Thomas, and Charles Baden-Fuller, "Competitive Groups as Cognitive Communities: The Case of Scottish Knitwear Manufacturers," *Journal of Management Studies* 26, no. 4 (1989): 397–416. For an accessible and comprehensive discussion of mental models, see Constantinos C. Markides, *All the Right*

Moves (Boston: Harvard Business School Press, 2000), especially pages 27–48.

6. The broad definition of resources to include tangible and intangible assets draws on the resource-based view of the firm. See B. Wernerfelt, "A Resource-Based View of the Firm," *Strategic Management Journal 5*, no. 2 (1984): 171–180; and J. Barney, "Firm Resources and Sustained Competitive Advantage," *Journal of Management* 17, no. 1 (1991): 99–120.

7. For a discussion of how relationships with external parties influence organizational behavior, see Jeffrey Pfeffer and Gerald R. Salancik, *The External Control of Organizations* (New York: Harper & Row, 1978) and Jeffrey H. Dyer and Harbir Singh, "The Relational View: Cooperative Strategy and Sources of Interorganizational Competitive Advantage," *Academy of Management Review* 23 (1988): 660–679.

8. For a useful overview of the role of culture, see Edgar H. Schein, "Culture: The Missing Concept in Organizational Studies," *Administrative Science Quarterly* 41, no. 2 (1996): 229–240; and Michael L. Tushman and Charles A. O'Reilly III, *Winning Through Innovation* (Boston: Harvard Business School Press, 1997), especially pages 99–154.

CHAPTER NINE

1. For a fuller discussion of the risks of long-term vision in unpredictable markets, see Donald N. Sull, "The Tunnel Vision Trap," *Financial Times*, August 4, 2004.

2. All quotations in this chapter come from interviews with company executives, as detailed in the appendix.

Donald N. Sull is an Associate Professor of Management Practice at the London Business School and was formerly an assistant professor at the Harvard Business School. He has authored or coauthored over fifty articles, book chapters, and case studies, as well as four books, including *Revival of the Fittest: Why Good Companies Go Bad* (Harvard Business School Press, 2003), which was named a finalist for the Academy of Management's George R. Terry Award for Outstanding Management Book and translated into eight languages. He serves as an adviser to firms in the United States, Europe, and Asia. Before entering academia, he worked as a consultant with McKinsey & Company and as a member of the management team that restructured the Uniroyal-Goodrich Tire Company.

Sull's research has won awards that include the George S. Dively Award for outstanding dissertation, the Newcomen Prize for the best paper in business history, and inclusion in the *Academy of Management Best Paper Proceedings*. He received his AB, MBA, and doctorate from Harvard University.